W9-BNC-707

Raising Careful, Confident Kids in a Crazy World

Raising Careful, Confident Kids in a Crazy World

PAULA STATMAN

previously titled **On the Safe Side**
©1995 HarperPerennial

 Piccolo Press

RAISING CAREFUL, CONFIDENT KIDS IN A CRAZY WORLD. Copyright © 1999 by Paula Statman. All rights reserved. Printed in the United States of America. No part of this book may be used or reproduced in any manner whatsoever without written permission except in the case of brief quotations embodied in critical articles and reviews. For information address Piccolo Press, 484 Lake Park Ave. #101, Oakland, CA 94610.

SECOND EDITION

Designed by Margaret Copeland

ISBN 0-9640042-2-4

To my husband, Alan,
whose abiding love has
sustained me,
for our daughter, Lauren,
and
for "Gail"

Contents

Preface

I have always loved kids. A friend of mine once said to me, "Children come easily to you." Whether it's that they come easily to *me* or that I go easily to *them*, I've always chosen to work with kids in one way or another. In high school, I worked as a baby-sitter, a Sunday school teacher, and a camp counselor. It seemed like the logical next step was to get a degree in elementary education. However, once in the classroom, I realized that I was more interested in the students who *weren't* doing well—the kids who seemed unhappy or unmotivated. That led me to change course and ultimately to earn a master's degree in clinical social work.

For the first ten years of my career, I developed my expertise as a psychotherapist and family life educator, working with children and adults in a number of settings. It was satisfying work, both personally and professionally, as well as being difficult and challenging. During this period of my life, I married my husband and gave birth to my daughter.

Having a daughter created profound changes in my life. As any parent will tell you, once your baby is born, you're in for a few surprises, no matter how prepared you think you are. Well, that certainly was true for me.

During my pregnancy I assumed that what I'd learned in

working with children would give me confidence as a parent. But when my daughter was born, and I saw how small and helpless she was, suddenly I felt unprepared. What if something happened to her? With all of my heart I wanted to protect her from harm. Would I be able to keep her safe? I felt ferociously protective one minute and tremendously vulnerable the next. Nothing I had learned before becoming a parent prepared me for these intense and conflicting emotions.

A few months after my daughter was born, I was asked to speak about personal safety at a community meeting. On that particular evening, a father gave a speech I'll never forget. The man's son had been abducted and was still missing after three years. The father's pain could be felt by every person in that room. Overcome by grief and rage, he warned parents to protect their children from "the perverts and pedophiles who roam our streets." His impassioned plea to stop criminals from "snatching our children" left people stunned and silent. Some parents were crying.

Next came a police officer who passed out fact sheets and talked about the "frightening statistics" surrounding sex offenders and abductors. People shook their heads in disbelief as the officer described several crimes that had never been solved. In each case, a child had been brutally murdered after being coaxed from a park or a shopping mall. After several more explicit accounts of rape and murder, it was my turn to speak.

As I stood there looking out at those parents, I wondered what I could possibly say that would reassure them. Would they be able to hear me, given how deeply the words of my colleagues had affected them? People looked afraid. I understood their fear; I was having a hard time managing my own.

On my way home that night, I couldn't stop thinking about those parents. Their faces were permanently etched in my mind. I knew that some of my colleagues believed that scare tactics were the fastest way to get people's attention, but I doubted that anybody in that audience felt better prepared to talk to their kids after having heard those horror stories. I seriously questioned what making parents afraid had to do with improving the way they protected their children.

That community meeting wasn't the first time I had seen parents "educated" this way. I had participated in two panels in which the presenters had used outright scare tactics. Detailed accounts of how young victims were raped, mutilated, and murdered were presented in the name of raising public awareness. In an overzealous effort to bring child safety to parents' attention—they had used fear to shake people out of their complacency.

In the early 1980s, the general attitude toward parents seemed to be, "You bet there's something to be afraid of! Here's a list of safety tips. Go home and teach them." I felt this approach disregarded the needs of parents. If we expected them to teach safety effectively, we should at least give them the same kind of information and support we were giving their children.

I decided to find out what training materials were available to parents. At that time personal-safety information was just being developed. Much of it consisted of fact sheets and lists of safety tips. I could find only one book for parents that dealt with how to talk with children about personal safety. And none of the available literature offered help in coping with parents' fears.

Overall, the aim was to get information to children through picture books, activity books, and audiotapes. Most personal-safety books and tapes had to be ordered through the mail. So, unless parents came across the right catalog or brochure, they were out of luck in finding material to use for home teaching. I concluded that there were two reasons for the lack of training materials for parents: (1) the personal-safety movement was just gaining momentum and (2) at that time, personal-safety education was being taught by "experts," not by parents.

During that period some preschools and elementary schools began offering personal-safety training to their students. Usually it was a one-hour safety session presented once a year. As any teacher will tell you, children learn and remember information over time, through repetition and practice. One hour was simply too short to be effective. By combining a "booster-shot" approach with claims that children would now be safe in *any* situation, these early programs created a false sense of security in children and parents. In addition, there was a lack of uniform training among safety experts and the quality of programs varied widely.

After I finished my research, I felt strongly that if children were going to get ongoing personal-safety training, parents were going to have to provide it. And parents were going to need much more information to be effective. They would need the same information that personal-safety experts had. And, to tell you the truth, the experts were still learning.

When people ask me why I created a personal-safety program for parents, I tell them there are two reasons. First, when I entered the field, educators expected parents to teach personal safety, but didn't empower them to do so. Second, I believed that parents could be extremely effective in teaching personal safety if their needs were taken into account. So I designed a program that offered parents information, support, and, most importantly, a way to teach personal safety that fit into their everyday lives.

A few months after I created the program, a local church asked me to speak before a group of parents. At that point, my ideas were still taking shape, but I had a title that, to me, said it all: *Raising Careful, Confident Kids in a Crazy World.* I liked it because I wanted parents to start thinking that it was possible to teach kids to be *both* confident and careful.

My workshop hit home with parents, teachers, counselors, and child-care professionals. Soon I had workshops scheduled all over California, and within a year I was presenting programs nationally. In 1991, I was asked to develop an audiotape and workbook version of the workshop. A proud moment came in 1993 when the audiotape program won a Parents' Choice Approved honor for best books and tapes for parents.

Today, I present *Raising Careful, Confident Kids in a Crazy World* to corporations, government agencies, and professional organizations, as well as church and parents' groups. I lecture extensively around the United States, speaking about personal safety and related issues.

As I put the finishing touches on my book, I find myself thinking about how it came to be. I see this book as a sign of our times, a response to the demand from parents and other concerned adults for useful, practical information. Today's parents, for example, can review safety tips for children with the push of a button. Home-computer users with on-line information services can call up "Eight Safety Tips for Children" or access data banks of missing children. The arrival of child safety on the information superhighway tells us we have traveled far since the early days of leaflets and community forums. I'm also encouraged by the nationwide legislative activity aimed at protecting our children. After an all-out effort that took more than a decade, child safety is finally on everyone's mind.

This book reflects my commitment to parents and to my belief that we can teach our children to be safe, strong, and street-smart. Contained in its pages is much of what I learned as a child and what I'm still learning as a mother and a teacher of personal safety. While it has taken me only a few months to write my thoughts down, I've spent years collecting them. I hope they will be of value to you.

Oakland, California
June 1994

Acknowledgments

My journey in completing this book has been filled with wonderful friends, colleagues, and family who have provided me with emotional support along the way. It is a great pleasure to thank all the people who have meant so much to me.

I want to thank my parents, who provided me with the support and education to develop my goals and dreams. Thank you to Laurie Edwards, whose wisdom and friendship over the past twelve years has been invaluable. Her unflagging support and resolute belief in my abilities served as a beacon of light through many long nights of writing.

Julie O'Mara, my brilliant mentor, brought perspective and focus to my project in its early stages and generously continues to bring these gifts to our friendship. My sincere thanks go to Shirley Davalos, video producer and visionary, who knew *exactly* what to do at *exactly* the right moment to breathe life into this project. I will be forever grateful to her for introducing me to my literary agent. I must thank Ted Brooks, who helped me turn my original message into an audiotape that led to bigger and greater things. Many thanks also go to Keith Hatschek and Dave Porter, who were willing to take a risk on me long before they knew where this would lead.

I've had wonderful teachers who helped me develop as a

psychotherapist and family life educator. I am indebted to Alan Raas, who believed I would make a good family life educator and gave me the opportunity to develop my first programs. I thank Mona Key, who helped me grow as a consultant and showed me what a beautifully run school could do for children. And I must thank one of my early consultants, Shirley Cooper, who said to me in 1983, "Write it down."

Stephanie Gunning, Associate Editor at HarperCollins, has my deepest gratitude for her enthusiastic support and flexibility from the very beginning to the very end of this project. Her sensitive commentary helped bring this book to its final shape. I'm particularly indebted to Candice Fuhrman, my literary agent, whose professional wisdom has guided me every step of the way. Her insight and know-how got this project off the ground and truly gave it wings.

Gail Simpson and Dave Roberts, loyal friends, have my heartfelt thanks for patiently reading my material back in its earliest stages and for celebrating each step forward with me. To Susan Page, fellow author and colleague, I offer my deepest appreciation for her generosity and personal guidance. Also, thank you to Marcia Black, Suyin Stein, Susan Sugarman, Judy Muschel, Ann Glasser, Sherry Jordana, and many other dear friends and colleagues who respected my need for solitude while I was writing.

I'm thankful to those who advocate for and protect our children in Congress and on the streets. And I thank the hundreds of parents, educators, and professional colleagues who gave me valuable lessons in the challenges of modern family life.

To my sister, Gail, I owe tremendous thanks for teaching me about the process of healing more than any textbook could have. I thank my wonderful husband, whose patient understanding and love have sustained me through writing this book and all our years together. And I thank my daughter, Lauren, who inspires me to advocate for all children who need our protection.

How to Use This Book

This book is designed to give you a simple, practical approach to teaching personal safety. As your children grow from ages three through twelve, it will be a resource you can use again and again. I suggest that you read the book completely the first time through. Then, once you understand the concepts and are comfortable teaching the safety skills, use the book as a reference guide.

The first two chapters deal with change—how our society has changed and how the way we protect our children must also change. In chapter 3, you'll learn how to establish the foundation for teaching personal safety effectively; you'll learn how to establish open family communication and nurture your child's self-esteem. These two elements, combined with specific safety skills, turn *nice* kids into *safe* kids.

There may be points in your reading where you feel uncomfortable. Well, you're not alone. The topic of children's safety makes most parents uncomfortable. Just keep in mind that you *can* manage your fears and concerns. I'll show you how in chapter 4, when I discuss teaching personal safety without using scare tactics.

In chapter 5, you'll discover that what you already know about your kids—combined with learning how sex offenders operate—can be extremely helpful in teaching personal safety. You'll learn what safety skills to teach and when to teach them in chapter 6. The next three chapters are divided by age groups. Chapter 7 focuses on personal-safety skills for children ages three through five. Chapter 8 covers which safety skills to teach children six through nine years of age. And chapter 9 deals with personal-safety skills for preteens ten through twelve years old. These three chapters stress that the best gauge to use in determining what information to teach, apart from your child's age or grade level, is to consider your child's intellectual, emotional, and social maturity.

In chapter 10, you'll learn how to teach personal safety during your routines and normal activities. You'll develop a simple learning activity that won't take much preparation and will make your job a whole lot easier. Every activity is designed so that your children will not only remember safety information but *use* it. Also in this chapter you'll learn a time-saving technique that uses "teachable moments." By recognizing and using teachable moments, you'll make personal safety a natural and familiar part of your family life, and you won't need to find extra time in your busy schedule to teach personal-safety skills.

Chapter 11 deals with preparing preteens for the responsibilities and privileges they want. There are tips for evaluating how much independence they can safely handle, some street-smart safety tips, and some important skills to teach kids who are home alone. What to do if your child is missing or is sexually abused is the focus of chapter 12.

This book is your personal map. Your path is clearly marked and I'll be traveling with you as your guide. Thank you for taking this journey on behalf of all the children who need us to show them the way.

Introduction

If you're troubled by how to raise children safely in an increasingly unsafe world, you're not alone. As a therapist and family life educator, I see how parents worry about protecting their children. For the past twenty years I've worked with hundreds of parents, educators, and child-care professionals in all kinds of communities. Here are some of their typical questions and comments:

> "It makes me angry that we have to teach our children to be afraid of strangers."
> "My child is so frightened about all the kidnappings in the news, she practically won't leave the house anymore!"
> "What can my child do to protect himself?"
> "I want my children to have some freedom, but the world is so unsafe these days."

Do those concerns sound familiar? Everywhere I go, I hear how frustrated and vulnerable people are feeling about protecting our children. Nobody wants children to feel scared about walking down the street, but we're scared ourselves. Nobody wants children to grow up not trusting others, but we're not sure who they can trust.

How do we teach our kids to stay safe without communicating our own fears? Is it possible to show our concern without also sharing our anxieties? We want them to be careful—not fearful—but we're unsure how to instill a sense of caution without frightening them.

Recently I overheard a woman at a public phone talking with her teenager. The teen was asking permission to walk over to a friend's house. The mother asked the usual questions: "When will you be home?" "Who's going to be there?" But then, instead of signing off with a reminder like "Be home by dinnertime," she astonished me by ending the conversation with "Remember, don't get into any cars." Things certainly have changed.

We feel the impact of many changes in our lives. More and more I overhear conversations at the grocery store or at the movies—people shake their heads and say, "It's just not safe for kids anymore." Everyone is talking about the violence that surrounds our children. Perfect strangers commiserate about how hard it is to help our children feel secure, agreeing that what once felt like a natural responsibility of adulthood and parenthood now feels like a difficult burden.

News reports about the violence erupting on our streets alarm us every day. Our teachers and law enforcement officers are confronted with juvenile crime that is unprecedented in our country's history. Crime in all forms touches more people's lives on a daily basis. Just last month my husband and I were at our bank when we heard someone shout, "Everybody freeze!" We whirled around in stunned silence, trying to grasp what was happening. All eyes focused on a teenage boy wearing a kaleidoscope-colored hat. There was an endless, silent second. Then, incredibly, the boy broke into a grin and sauntered merrily through the lobby and out the door, his prank having achieved its desired results. I was astounded by this young man's bravado. Had a security officer been there and taken this kid seriously, we might have seen this headline the next day: SECURITY GUARD SHOOTS TEEN IN ROBBERY HOAX. The pranks we played as teenagers were not always harmless, but they seem benign compared to this one. When a fifteen-year-old boy behaves so fearlessly, so recklessly, it makes me afraid for our future.

According to the director of the Institute for Child, Adolescent & Family Studies in New York City, Ava Siegler, Ph.D., "today's children, exposed so early to the temptations of modern life, are less able than ever to say no to drugs, to alcohol, to sex, to crime." In her book *What Should I Tell the Kids?*, she cites an increase in learning disabilities, juvenile violence, early drug and alcohol abuse, and childhood depression and suicide. With the serious deterioration among our youth, I see no choice but to aggressively invest our energies in the young people today who will be the adults and parents of tomorrow.

Siegler cites increases in family violence, drug and alcohol addiction, divorce, the spread of stress-related diseases, and parental child abuse, both physical and sexual. This means, for instance, that even children's own homes can no longer be seen as safe havens. It means that we cannot distance abusers from ourselves by simply regarding them as "bad" or "mad" or as criminally insane. And it means that parents cannot take for granted that they would know if something dreadful were happening to their own child. We don't welcome these signs of our times, but we must face them nevertheless. It is essential that we educate ourselves and remain alert for clues that our children are being mistreated.

From ages three to twelve, when so much personality and character development takes place, our responsibilities as parents can seem overwhelming. At that stage children are just beginning to move outside of the family circle, and they do so with a sense of wonder and curiosity. They often come to us for explanations of what they have seen. With so many problems in our world and on our streets, it is easy to see how we might overshadow their natural exuberance with our own fears. How do we answer their questions?

By following the steps in this book, you'll be able to answer their questions and learn how to teach the essential safety skills and information that will protect your children. I'll help you understand what to tell your kids and when and how to tell them. You'll recognize the crucial difference between teaching children to be careful and teaching them to be fearful. You'll get practical tools for showing your children how to be alert and aware of their surroundings, how to identify potentially unsafe or suspicious-looking situations, and how to respond to them safely. And last, but not least, you'll gain some peace of mind.

Without a doubt, raising safe, strong, and street-smart kids is heroic and hard work. And you—as your child's most important teacher—may feel a deep sense of responsibility about doing your job well. I wrote this book so that you wouldn't have to do it alone. I firmly believe that we can all become confident, skilled teachers of personal safety.

In this book, I'll suggest ways to talk about personal safety that have worked with the hundreds of children and parents I've known—ways that have worked with my own daughter. Despite the fact that crime in our society is escalating and that we, as parents, must respond accordingly, I believe that what I've written here will stand the test of time.

I write from the perspective of both a mother and a daughter, of a professional and a concerned citizen. I write from the perspective of someone who grew up in a small town in the Midwest, lived in several midsize communities, and spent seven years in one of the most diverse cities in the world—San Francisco. However, different cultures and ethnicities have distinct parenting styles and customs, and I cannot guarantee that my points will always align with your particular way of caring for your children. I respect that you may disagree with some of my ideas, but I hope that you will keep an open mind as you read.

Most of all, I want to thank you and congratulate you for taking the time to learn how to become the best teacher of personal safety you can be. I hope it will be a valuable investment of your energy. It's my sincere wish that the information in this book will empower you, your children, and your generations to come.

Raising Careful, Confident Kids in a Crazy World

CHAPTER 1

Protecting Children Today

Myths and Memories

Remember the days when you played "Kick the Can" in the street after dark, days when your parents didn't think twice about letting you play alone in your own backyard? We never dreamed that our children would grow up in a country so plagued with crime that they would miss out on these simple freedoms of childhood.

But now we are being told to prepare our children for a different world, a world in which child-related crimes and violence are commonplace. Our society and family structures have drastically changed. So have the politics and the economy of the world around us.

Today we are faced with new and unexpected challenges of child raising—stepparenting, single parenthood, AIDS, drug abuse, violence, and more. Our kids are facing extraordinary pressures at a time when our abilities as parents to protect them seem considerably diminished.

For most of us, becoming a parent is a major transition. One of the joys we look forward to is sharing the best of our own childhoods with our children. Then we find that there is barely any resemblance between the world we grew up in and the world we have created—and this feels unacceptable. We long for the "good old days." And we still struggle to accept that protecting our children today means something very different than it did thirty years ago.

A friend of mine, a single parent, laments about her life in the city—about how her son has all the freedom and independence of a "pet-store parakeet," and how he practically chains himself to his bike when he goes out for fear it will be stolen. Though I grew up in a small town and she in a city, we have shared memories of going everywhere on our bicycles—to the library, our friends' houses, the park—and returning home at dinnertime to doors that were always unlocked.

Both of us had a sense growing up that our world as children was safe enough for us to have a life separate from the adults. As children we felt securely anchored in our community and in our neighborhoods, free to cut through backyards, take shortcuts, and accept a cookie from practically anyone who would offer one.

We were safe in that world partly because everyone in our neighborhoods kept an eye out for everyone else. Much of what keeps us feeling safe and confident as adults developed in us during that time in our lives.

When we look beyond the sentimental glow that most childhoods eventually acquire in our memories, we realize that the world of our childhood did have its share of the grotesque, simply because the world always does.

Childhoods today—urban, suburban, or rural—are neither the childhoods we had nor the childhoods we would have invented for our children. Every child is of his or her time, and a "real" childhood is the one our children are living now. We need to help our kids learn how to gauge what's safe and to provide opportunities for them to be as free as possible. With any luck at all, our children will fondly remember their childhoods thirty years from now.

What Our Parents Never Told Us

Children raised in the fifties and sixties were taught to strictly obey authority figures. Saying no to an adult was considered rude and disrespectful. We now know that many of these "respectful" children also were victims of sexual abuse.

Beginning in the 1970s adults who had been sexually abused as children came forward and broke the taboo about discussing "private family matters." They opened a collective box of childhood horrors and forced us to look into it. We were shocked to learn that sexual abuse of children was a serious problem thirty or forty years ago, just as it is today, and that in many cases it became a family legacy passed on from one generation to the next. When we were growing up, fewer people reported child-related crimes. Today, crimes against children are reported across America, in small towns, large cities, and rural areas, in churches and schools, and on every social and economic level.

As a society we still struggle with the fact that most children are abused by someone they know, often a trusted family friend or a beloved relative. We are shocked to learn that principal child abusers are often parents, stepparents, and live-in lovers, women as well as men. This betrayal of love and friendship angers us. We don't quite know how to explain this truth to our children, particularly when it wasn't something that was commonly discussed when we were growing up. It is an uncomfortable truth we'd prefer not to face.

In my small midwestern town, for example, a fourth-grade classmate was molested by the mortician whose funeral home was located directly across from our school. The girl had told a friend who then whispered this news all the way around the playground. The adults must have found out, because I remember the police were involved. As kids, we were given very few facts, so we used our overactive imaginations to fill in the missing details during recess. We had animated and fantasy-filled discussions about what the police were going to do to this bad man.

Looking at this classmate through the wide eyes of a child, I mostly wondered why she would want to play at a funeral parlor in the first place. Didn't she know there were dead people there?! In other words, I missed the point. Because teachers, police, and parents didn't interpret or explain what had happened to my classmate, I didn't know *what* I was supposed to be concerned about. So I moved on from that incident, taking with me a newfound fear of funeral parlors and nothing in the way of useful information.

One summer the children in my neighborhood were totally convinced that we were being stalked by a "phantom kidnapper" who drove a gold Volkswagen "beetle" and who, according to unreliable sources, would snatch up unsuspecting children. I don't know if this rumor was founded on a local incident or whether we made it up. But once again, without an adult to interpret and explain, our imaginations ran wild. Maybe we were just bored and needed a little excitement. We certainly got it. All summer, just the mere sight of a gold car sent kids into hysterics. It was irrelevant that no abductor in his right mind would force a child into a minuscule car that puttered along, an easy mark for any police in pursuit. That the actual sighting of this would-be kidnapper was never confirmed didn't matter either. Left to our own devices, we busily fanned the flames of our childhood fear with tall tales and false rumors.

In retrospect, our childhood fears seem lightweight compared to what our children grapple with today. Looking back, perhaps our ignorance allowed us to remain children a little longer. We didn't have much information, and neither we nor our parents talked openly about such things.

Today, as adults and parents we struggle with hard facts and alarming statistics. We can't afford to take the same risks our parents took. We can't hide our heads in the sand, and we can't "make it all better." We must educate our children about the world they live in honestly, carefully, and compassionately.

The New Protective Parent

Parents today say they are raising their children with more restrictions, structure, and supervision than they grew up with. A steady increase nationwide in reports of violent crime has fueled parents' fears that their children might be abducted or molested—or simply fall into the wrong peer group.

To safeguard their children, many parents enroll them in supervised after-school activities such as team sports, Scouting, or latchkey programs. They impose strict curfews, forbid them from playing outside after dark, and require their children to check in regularly when they are off with friends. Children, in turn, find they have less time and opportunity to hop on a bike and sail away.

With fewer parents home full-time, schools have taken on more responsibility for child safety. School bus drivers no longer allow children to get off at different stops. Parents must come into the school building to pick up their children instead of waiting at the curb in their cars.

All of this seems a world away from the simple messages we got growing up. When we were children we heard warnings like "Don't talk to strangers," "Don't take candy from strangers," and "Don't get into a car with strangers." If you are like most adults I talk to, this was the full extent of our "personal-safety training." Parents in the fifties and sixties believed that these warnings would keep us safe. Soon the next generation of parents arrived with the same inadequate information. Our streets had changed but our way of preparing our children hadn't.

As parents today we must understand the potential dangers our children face. We must see our neighborhoods and streets for what they are and prepare our children to navigate them safely. Today's children must be taught specific prevention strategies for a wider variety of potential dangers. We must learn to walk a thin line between the exposure of our children to life's possibilities and the protection of our children from life's burdens. And we must empower children with the message that they can be both confident *and* careful.

Striking a Healthy Balance

What does protecting children mean? Does it mean constantly being with them to keep them out of harm's way? If that's what you believe, you've probably learned that it's not possible beyond a certain age. And yet, the wish to keep our children safe is very strong. Some parents react by overprotecting their children, while others grant too much freedom, holding on to the illusion that nothing's going to happen to *their* child. Both extremes result in children being *more* vulnerable, just the opposite of what parents are trying to accomplish.

Overprotected children, for example, are not allowed to develop their own instincts and judgment, so they don't develop the skills to recognize unsafe or suspicious situations. They never develop a "sixth sense" about people or their surroundings. Overprotected children doubt their abilities and judgment, and depend too heavily on adults for guidance and information. As a result they are more susceptible to overtures from both well-intentioned and not-so-well-intentioned people.

Parents overprotect children partly out of their own need to feel in control and, in some cases, out of their need to feel powerful. Often this pattern of overprotecting starts when their children are becoming more independent. To ward off the feeling that they are no longer the center of their children's lives, or to quiet their fears about their children making more independent decisions, parents unwittingly undermine children's self-esteem and increase their feeling of helplessness. Helplessness and low self-esteem will not protect a child in a potentially dangerous situation. In fact, these are the very qualities that contribute to children being victimized.

In too many instances, I know of young people who rebel against too-restrictive rules to prove that their parents' fears are unfounded. None of us wants to make our children feel so incompetent that they would try something foolish to prove us wrong, yet offering more protection than the child really needs can trigger this kind of risky behavior. If, in order to feel more powerful or important, you disqualify your child's ability to use critical thinking and make good choices, you may be setting the stage for him to become a teenager who acts out.

As our children move toward adulthood, like it or not, we

will have *less and less* influence on them. That's because as they grow their world expands to include new people with many different views and ideas. They must find out who they are, separate and apart from us. And, in order to support their journey from dependent children to competent adults, we must give them some room to grow up and away from us. By preparing children to be more independent and by allowing them to have the *hundreds* of chances they will need to practice their independence, we are doing our jobs as parents.

Now let's look at the flip side of overprotection: allowing children too much freedom, assigning them too much responsibility, and exposing them to too much too soon. Unlike parents who overprotect their children, highly permissive parents tend to be unrealistic about their children's ability to learn from "trial and error."

I recall the news story of a woman whose baby drowned while her nine-year-old son was baby-sitting. The boy, who had been left in charge while the mother was at work, was giving the baby a bath. According to the report, the mother was on a waiting list for child care, and had routinely left her young son and baby with relatives while she worked and went to school. It was unclear why she didn't drop off her children at a relative's home that day and instead chose to leave the nine-year-old in charge.

This tragedy and many other less dramatic incidents illustrate that a child's ability to handle responsibility should be evaluated separately from—not in conjunction with—a parent's needs. "Just this once" kind of thinking is risky and often leads to failure. In some cases, it can be disastrous.

When one four-year-old kept begging his mother to be allowed to walk down to a neighbor's to play, she gave in. Tragically, that was the last time she ever saw him. It's been my experience that a lot of parents, including myself, find it hard to say no when our children are whining, throwing a tantrum, pleading, or being just plain cute. It's important to remember that kids spend a great deal of time and energy on finding ways to get us to say yes. It's their right as children to do so. But it's our right and responsibility to be strong enough to say "NO!"

Imagine the potential danger of allowing a small child who can't tell the difference between red pills and cinnamon candies to have access to a medicine cabinet because he "knows not to put things in his mouth." Remember the national scandal caused by the couple who left their two children, both under the age of twelve, at home while they went on vacation? They later lost custody of their children.

Errors in judgment like these are all too common. All of the decisions discussed above were filled with rationalizations or misinformation. The parent with the open medicine cabinet believed her preschooler had the discipline and understanding of a much older child. The mother of the four-year-old believed her son would be safe since the neighbor lived "just down the block." And the rationalizations of the couple who abandoned their children constituted neglect and child endangerment. While these cases may seem extreme, they make a point about what goes into our decisions to either protect or expose our children to potential danger.

Let's use an example from everyday life. Think about what it takes for the average ten-year-old to walk to school safely on his own. Consider how your child rates in these skill areas:

- Awareness of his surroundings
- Ability to safely interact with strangers
- Ability to follow rules (e.g., don't take shortcuts, cross the street at the crosswalk)
- Ability to handle peer pressure/not respond to dares

How did your child do? If your child doesn't have all of these skills, there are three things you can do: (1) have him walk with a safety-conscious friend; (2) drive him to and from school; or (3) practice these skills by walking to school with him. One option I don't recommend is allowing your child to walk alone, at least not until these skills are fully developed. Also, consider your child's environment and the potential dangers he may encounter. What may be an appropriate freedom in one neighborhood may be inappropriate in another.

To keep our children safe, we must recognize when to:

a. Protect them from the situation because it is beyond their abilities
b. Prepare them for the situation because it is something they can learn about and will need to handle, or
c. Practice with them because they are not yet competent to handle the situation without supervision

In order to know which tactic to use, you must know something about your child and her abilities. You don't get that kind of information from a book. You get it from being a good observer, from noticing your child's strengths and weaknesses, and from keeping track of her progress over time. In chapter 4, I'll show you how to use this information to decide what safety skills and information your child needs to learn.

Protecting vs. Projecting

So much of what we project onto our children tends to be "unfinished business" in ourselves. For instance, if a father was fearful and anxious as a boy, he may try to raise a fearless son. Each time his son displays his courage, the father showers him with praise. Over time, the boy learns that showing bravery—or in its absence, bravado—is wiser than showing fear. The boy consistently tries to act courageous even when he doesn't feel that way. He gets trapped into acting out a role in order to please his father. And while the father basks in the glow of his son's bravery, the boy soon learns to hide any signs of vulnerability or weakness and pays a high emotional price for doing so.

A mother, deprived of attention as a little girl, grows up feeling that she is unlovable. She conveys her sense of worthlessness to her daughter by, in turn, ignoring her. Although the mother very much intends to be a caring and attentive parent, she is unconsciously repeating the cycle of emotional neglect from her own childhood.

Being conscious about our childhoods and how they get stirred up as we raise our own children allows us to rethink how to handle situations that were handled poorly in the past. We may need new skills and information to improve on our parents' behavior. We may feel awkward at first with words and behavior we never knew before. But learning and growing as parents is the only way we can guarantee that our children won't play out the rigidly determined roles and old scripts from our own childhoods. When we are aware of painful childhood memories and try to resolve them, we are less likely to re-create them in our new families.

Let's look at some of the views we may carry into parenthood that can get in the way of protecting our children. Sometimes parents feel that the sooner they expose their children to adult experiences the better off they'll be. With this kind of thinking, there's the risk of overexposure, that is, telling children and showing children too much about adult life too soon. Overexposing children to adult matters can be overwhelming for them. Without the intellectual or emotional maturity to effectively deal with what they are seeing or hearing, they can become stressed or traumatized.

I remember one family I worked with many years ago who carried this belief to the extreme. The father repeatedly told me that the sooner his nine-year-old son was initiated into "a man's world," the sooner he would become a man. Nothing I said could dissuade him from overstimulating his son with stories of his sexual prowess. Ultimately the father's "pep talks" led to sexual acting out involving both parents, and the boy was removed from the home.

Parents who grew up in dysfunctional families often have distorted ideas about child-rearing practices. When their beliefs about child rearing are based on having had to grow up too fast, there's the risk of "parentifying" children, meaning that parents—unwittingly, in most cases—turn their children into miniature grown-ups. Without being aware of it, they may actively interfere with their children's need to function as children.

I have seen many adults over the years who as children took care of younger siblings because of a parent's illness, death, or incapacity. Their carefree days of childhood were cut short and replaced by years of being responsible for others long before they could adequately care for themselves. At the same time these parents make a conscious effort to give their children a real childhood, they still grieve over the childhoods they never had.

I see adult children of alcoholic parents who expect their children to "overfunction" just as they had to in order for their families to survive. Parents unknowingly burden their children with their troubles, sorrows, and pain. Family crises, drug and alcohol problems, and a pervasive lack of emotional security threaten to overwhelm their children. In some cases, these parents must also break the cycle of physical abuse they grew up with. Because of strong ambivalent feelings about exposing—rather than protecting—their children, adult children of alcoholics must work harder to create an appropriate psychological and emotional environment. The unconscious need to give their children "exactly what they got" can sometimes get in the way.

If these issues are getting in the way of your being the kind of parent you want to be, then I urge you to get help. Entering therapy yourself or with your family is good insurance against your personal history repeating itself. By learning new ways to nurture yourself and your children, you will heal old wounds and enjoy parenting more.

How Do You Protect Your Child?

In this section, you'll be asked to respond to five different situations in which you are asked to decide which approach would be best. If you don't have a child in each of the age groups represented, try to imagine how you might respond in that particular instance. After you complete the questions, read the two sections that follow: "What Your Answers Mean" and "Discussion."

1. Someone you don't know approaches you and your three-
   year-old, compliments you about how cute your child is,
   and then reaches out to touch him or her. What do you do?
   a) Shout loudly, "Get away from my child right now!"
   b) Say nothing.
   c) Say, "I know you mean no harm, but please don't touch
   my child."

2. Your seven-year-old wants to play in the front yard by
   herself. What do you do?
   a) Let her play alone.
   b) Let her play with a friend in the yard as long as she and
   the friend can follow the safety rules.
   c) Let her play outside while you supervise her.

3. Your baby-sitter just canceled and you have an important
   appointment to go to in an hour. Your ten-year-old has
   offered to baby-sit his four- and seven-year-old brothers.
   What do you do?
   a) Call an adult friend or teenager to come over. Let your
   ten-year-old baby-sit with supervision.
   b) Tell your ten-year-old he is too young and find another
   baby-sitter.
   c) Let your ten-year-old baby-sit the two younger children.

4. Your eight-year-old seems particularly nervous about an
   upcoming overnight at a relative's home. What do you do?
   a) Ask him to tell you what he's worried about, and if he
   can't, reassure him that he will have a good time once
   he gets there.
   b) Cancel the overnight on the basis of his reactions.
   c) If it's unusual for him to worry about an overnight,
   respect his feelings and let him make the choice about
   going.

5. Your eleven-year-old wants to walk to a nearby store with
   a friend. What do you do?
   a) Let her go because you want your daughter to know
   you trust her and have confidence in her good judgment.

b) Tell her that she's much too young to go to the store by herself.

c) Base your decision on how well she's handled similar privileges in the past, how well the two friends behave when unsupervised, and how safe your neighborhood is.

The best answers are 1c, 2b, 3a, 4c, and 5c.

WHAT YOUR ANSWERS MEAN

If you chose one or more of these answers—1b, 2a, 3c, 4a, 5a—watch for these patterns in the way you protect your children:

- Expecting too much too soon
- Allowing your child to try new experiences without enough preparation
- Giving in because your child manipulates you or protests your limits
- Denying your child's feelings due to your own needs

If you chose one or more of these answers—1a, 2c, 3b, 4b, 5b—watch for these patterns in the way you protect your children:

- Expecting too little from your child, even after he has shown an interest in accepting more responsibility
- Telling your child why it's not safe for her to do something even after she has demonstrated her ability to act responsibly
- Setting too restrictive limits on the basis of your fears

DISCUSSION

In the first example, where the friendly stranger reaches out to touch your child, you may have been tempted to choose "Say nothing" for your answer. Some parents feel that as long as they are supervising the situation, it's OK. Others feel awkward about speaking up because their child seems to enjoy the attention. And, especially when you are dealing with an older person, he or she is likely to say, "Oh, it's all right, I'm a grandparent!"

While you can be sensitive to the fact that older people were brought up in a time when violence was not so widespread and children were taught to be friendly, you should not permit *any* stranger to touch your young child. Here's why: If you allow that friendly stranger to touch your child, you're teaching her that it's OK for people to touch her *if they act friendly.*

The problem with encouraging this kind of thinking is that the majority of sex offenders entice children with *friendship or affection.* As parents we can't afford to give our children the message that letting a friendly stranger touch them is OK. Teach your child that appropriate strangers do *not* touch children. Tell your child, "We don't let strangers hug you, even friendly people like the man we just saw." And, if you are concerned about offending well-intended strangers, you could explain to them, "We're teaching him how to behave with strangers."

Stepping in or speaking up may take some practice. And your willingness to be a little uncomfortable allows your child to feel secure and protected. It helps to remember three things. First, you're trying to teach your child that she shouldn't let strangers touch her. Second, you're demonstrating how to set limits and personal boundaries, a skill your young child learns by watching and copying you.

Third, by intervening, you're telling her that friendly behavior from adults does not entitle them to touch her. You want her to get a consistent message that appropriate behavior from strangers includes a smile, a brief or friendly greeting, but nothing more. You want your child to learn to expect appropriate treatment from strangers. Then, if for some reason there comes a time when she isn't treated appropriately, her "inner alarm" will go off and she'll be more likely to respond in a self-protective way.

Using a common incident—like the one where a stranger tries to touch your child—to teach a safety concept is what I call using a "teachable moment": When a natural opportunity to teach or reinforce a safety rule presents itself, you take advantage of it. Throughout each day there will be spontaneous opportunities to teach your children safety information or practice a skill. By having safety conversations during normal routines and activities, you make personal safety a natural and familiar part of your family life. And teachable moments fit easily into your busy schedule! We'll talk more about teachable moments in chapter 10.

In the second example, your seven-year-old wants to play in the front yard by herself. I recommend that instead you invite a trustworthy buddy and let the two play together. The buddy system is always safer, provided the other child doesn't take foolish risks. If that just isn't possible, a child of this age needs someone looking out for her while she is outside. With my own daughter, I often take the newspaper outside to read or I'll sit on the stoop and pay my bills while she plays nearby.

When you have a willing—but not yet able—ten-year-old who volunteers to baby-sit, as you do in the third example, by no means do you want to discourage him. But I have yet to meet a ten-year-old I would place in charge of two small children. They are excellent candidates, however, for being "Mother's Helpers," which provides them with the supervision they need. Then, around age twelve, enroll them in a baby-sitting course that will round out their training and prepare them for the responsibility of managing children alone.

So often, protecting our children means respecting their feelings on *their* terms, not ours. That's what I suggest you do in the fourth example, when your eight-year-old balks at staying overnight at a relative's home. I recommend that you respect your child's feelings even if he can't back them up with facts or details. When an invitation to visit a beloved friend causes your child to be uncharacteristically nervous or resistant, don't get annoyed, get curious!

Let's say you've been using a new baby-sitter, a teenage boy. He seems nice, and your seven-year-old daughter seems very happy and comfortable each time you leave her in his care. One morning at breakfast, however, following an evening when he took care of your daughter, she is moody and irritable. You find out that she didn't go to bed too late, and she's not sick, so you're wondering why she's in such a bad mood. You ask her if she had a good time with the sitter and she says, "Sort of." You ask, "What do you mean, 'sort of'?" and she suddenly gets very angry and shouts, "Can't you hear me?! I said, 'sort of'!" and stomps out of the kitchen.

Though you may feel like you should call her back into the kitchen and have her apologize for answering you so rudely, you would be wise not to conclude quickly that what you're seeing is just bad manners—it's better to get on the phone to the sitter. That's exactly what the father in this situation does: He calls Aaron, the sitter who took care of his daughter, Amber, last night.

Aaron: Hello?

Father: Hi, Aaron?

Aaron: Yes?

Father: This is Amber's father. Listen, I was wondering if you could tell me a little more about how things went last night.

Aaron: Everything was fine. Amber and I made popcorn and watched videos. She beat me in Go Fish and then went to bed about nine o'clock. She was in a great mood the whole time.

Father: Well, I thought she enjoyed having you take care of her, but now this morning she seems upset and I can't get much out of her.

Aaron: Really? She seemed OK last night.

Father: Yeah, that's what's so confusing. Anyway, we'll work it out. Thanks for your help.

Aaron: Sure. Hope she'll be OK. Bye . . .

Father: Good-bye.

What should he do with this information? The sitter said things went great, but his daughter isn't *acting* like things went great. He knows there's something bothering her, something the girl can't explain. The father chooses to approach Amber to find out if she was mistreated by the baby-sitter, rather than assume that she just "got up on the wrong side of the bed" that morning.

Father: Honey, I noticed how upset you got with me a moment ago. I'm sorry if you felt like I was asking a lot of questions, but I get the feeling that something happened last night when Aaron was here that you didn't like. Is there something you need to tell me?

Amber: I told you already.

Father: I heard what you said. And if something else is wrong, whatever it is, it sure looks like it's hard to talk about it.

(Amber silently nods her head yes, looking down.)

Father: OK, then, we're going to make it easier. I'll be a detective and try to guess. If you can give me any clues along the way, that would really help. Did Aaron do anything or say anything to you that has upset you? Or has he done something that he's told you not to tell anyone about?

Amber: Kind of . . .

Father: Nobody is supposed to tell children to keep secrets from their parents and that *includes* baby-sitters.

Amber: (Anxiously) But he told me something bad would happen to Tiger if I told you! (Tiger is their cat.)

Father: Aaron was afraid he would be in trouble if you told us, so he told you a scary lie to keep you quiet. It's OK for you to tell me. I won't let anyone hurt Tiger.

Amber: Well, OK . . . um, he asked me if I wanted to play being married and I said yes. Then he said we should both take our clothes off and get into my bed. I told him I didn't want to take off my clothes and he got mad at me. That's when he said he would hurt Tiger if anyone found out about our game.

Father: No wonder you were so upset this morning. It was brave of you to tell me. You did the right thing.

Amber: Well, now Aaron will be mad at me because I told you.

Father: I know you like Aaron, but Aaron broke some very important baby-sitting rules. Baby-sitters should never ask you to get undressed or play games where they touch your private parts or you touch theirs. This is Aaron's problem, not yours. I'm going to talk to his mother and see that he gets help.

Because the father was alert to changes in his daughter's behavior, he picked up her signal for help. Also, because he chose to accept his daughter's feelings—even though he didn't like her *behavior*—he was able to keep the communication open. He showed compassion and understanding and remained calm. He also gave her crucial information that should help protect her in the future.

By the way, this conversation may not be over. There's a good chance that more happened to Amber than she could tell her father about all at once. If the father discovers that there was more physical contact, then he needs to report the incident to the authorities and have his daughter examined by a physician. To help Amber recover from the incident, her father needs to lift any remaining burden and guilt and responsibility from her shoulders and place the responsibility for the incident with Aaron. In subsequent conversations, the father needs to reinforce the idea that teenagers and grown-ups are not supposed to play sex games with children.

This example clearly illustrates how we are more likely to protect our children if we respect our children's feelings, even if we don't have all the facts. Protecting our children means being a good observer of behavior and not distorting what we see or hear. When we use what we know about our children, when we put our own feelings aside, keep our eyes and ears open, and are willing to speak up and act on their behalf, we're much more able to protect them.

We can't protect children by hovering over them or by hoping for the best. We *can* protect them by using age-appropriate expectations, by not pushing them beyond their abilities, and by considering how well they can handle a situation before we say yes. In essence, we protect children by giving them the freedom they need to grow, one supervised step at a time.

Key Points

- Step in or speak up on your child's behalf.
- Know and use age-appropriate expectations.
- Respect your child's feelings, no matter how they are communicated.
- Grant freedom and responsibility on the basis of your child's demonstrated skills and abilities.
- Supervise your child until he or she is adequately prepared for more responsibility.
- Set limits clearly and firmly.

CHAPTER 2

That Was Then—This Is Now

According to FBI figures released in May 1999, crime plummeted nationwide for a record seventh straight year, declining 7 percent. Nationwide, homicides fell 8 percent from the previous year. Attorney General Janet Reno, the nation's top law enforcement officer said, "That means safer streets, fewer victims and greater peace of mind for all Americans."

So, why don't we have greater peace of mind?

When I speak to audiences around the country, one of the first questions I ask is, "At what rate have molestations and abductions increased in the past 20 years?" The vast majority of audiences call out numbers like 50%, 200%, even 300%. Few realize that the rate has remained relatively steady; it is reporting and media coverage that has increased dramatically. The "statistics" in their minds are driven by fear.

Who or what is responsible for fueling Americans' fears? Some experts and media critics point to television as the guilty party. "If it bleeds, it leads" has become the catch phrase for national and local news.

Broadcasts of crime stories have soared along with the public's fear of crime. From 1990 to 1995—a period when the FBI reported a 13 percent drop in the homicide rate—network news coverage of murder increased a whopping 336 percent, and that did not even include coverage of the O.J. Simpson case, according to the Center for Media and Public Affairs.

Another reason our fear keeps rising is this: long after crimes against children occur, the names, even faces, of victims linger. Twelve-year-old Polly Klaas is kidnapped from her Petaluma bedroom, then raped and murdered. Three-year-old Stephanie Kuhen is shot to death in a Los Angeles alley. Six-year-old beauty queen JonBenet Ramsey dies of strangulation in the small city of Boulder, Colorado.

Add to those lingering and disturbing memories more news stories, like the one about the teenager who sexually assaults and strangles an 11-year-old boy going door to door selling candy for charity.

"While memory fades over time, it gets kicked up every time you hear about a new crime that allows you to identify with the victim," said Alfred Blumstein, a criminology professor at Carnegie Mellon University. "Polly Klaas could have been any of our daughters, and that murder stirs up all our concerns for our daughters."

We remain emotionally resilient, even when barraged with disturbing images and stories. Beyond that point, it's easy to lose sight of what is true.

The Truth and Nothing But the Truth

While it may be tempting to tune out the truth in order to avoid feeling upset, there are some facts that every parent and concerned professional should know. These statistics and findings compel us to be more alert, aware, and committed to preparing our children for today's world. My purpose in presenting this information is not to scare you; rather, it is to help you examine conflicting facts that have made it difficult for you to know what to believe.

According to the U.S. Department of Justice, there are 250,000 to 500,000 pedophiles in the United States—a *pedophile* is an adult who sexually desires children and who seeks out children for the purpose of having sex. It is estimated that each pedophile will molest between 250 and 350 children in his or her lifetime. It is critical to remember that "75–85 percent of sex crimes against children are committed by someone the child knows, loves, or trusts." Molestation can start when children are infants; however, the most vulnerable years are between nine and twelve. An estimated one in four girls and one in eight boys are sexually abused before age eighteen. A new study reports those numbers may be as high as one in two girls and one in four boys.

In a study based on the largest survey ever conducted of state prison inmates, the Justice Department reported that two-thirds of sex offenders attacked children, and a third of these victims were offspring or stepchildren of their attackers.

David Beatty, acting executive director of the National Victims Center, a private advocacy group in Arlington, Virginia said, "The majority of sex crimes are committed against children because they are more helpless, easier targets and easier to intimidate into silence."

The study examined the abduction and murder of 600 children in more than 44 states. Although child abduction-murders are rare—only one-tenth of one percent of all murders nationwide—it found that 58 percent of abductions occurred within a quarter-mile of home. Typically, the perpetrators lived or regularly passed through the area where they abducted their victims.

This same study called for citizens to be aware of strangers and unusual behavior in their neighborhoods. What appears to be an adult coping with an unruly child might be more serious, the study said, since many child abductions are witnessed by people who do not realize that a crime is being committed.

Typical abductors are about 27 years old, white and unmarried, and most have prior arrests for violence or for crimes against children. Typical victims, by contrast, are usually white girls, about 11, often described as "normal kids" from middle class neighborhoods with stable families, the study said.

In 74 percent of the cases, the child was killed within three hours of being kidnapped. It is important to note that while most child abductions are committed by family and friends, most abductions that result in murder are committed by strangers—53%, the study said.

The most important recommendation from the study was for quick action. It took more than two hours for police to be notified of an abduction in 60 percent of the cases, and 74 percent of the children were killed within three hours of being kidnapped. Police need to conduct neighborhood canvasses immediately to find out where the child was last seen. The study also showed that the solvability rate dropped dramatically when police did not know the site where a victim was contacted by her abductor, but increased when they did.

Fear of Violence Rising Among Youth

In 1995, a national study was conducted by Kaiser Permanente and Children Now, a national child advocacy group. Young people—regardless of their age, region, or demographic group—cited violence, guns and gangs as the biggest threats in their lives.

"Children are losing their childhood," said Maryann O'Sullivan, director of special health initiatives for Children Now. "If a child has this level of fear about serious survival issues, then the time they should be spending playing and learning, they're using up being anxious. This can reduce their chance of growing into productive adults."

Random school shootings in comfortable-looking communities like Littleton, Colorado, where the worst school shooting in U.S. history took place on April 21, 1999, have shaken our country to its core. Although recent statistics show a decline in violence in our schools, between October 1997 and April 1999, seven shootings involving teachers and students made national headlines.

Experts speaking out in the wake of these tragedies said it was only a matter of time before violence of this magnitude happened. At the center of the debate is what led to these rampages.

Ken Dodge, director of the Center for Child and Family Policy at Duke University, who has been tracking 900 high-risk youngsters for as long as eight years says, "Sometimes you can see it coming." Not every violent child is alike, but there are clear risk factors—low-income families, dangerous neighborhood, overly harsh discipline, exposure to violence in the home—that can lock children into a hostile frame of mind as early as kindergarten or first grade.

Fortunately, the latest statistics also show that violence, in fact, is declining overall in U.S. schools. The problem is that the horrific events at Columbine High School and elsewhere suggest that "the face of violence may be changing," said Deborah Phillips, a developmental psychologist at the National Research Council. "This form of random shooting in public settings seems to be on the rise, and that's a huge worry," she said. "What is it that really triggers these events?"

Investigators are looking into mental-health social factors affecting the youngest children, even if the worst symptoms only emerge years later. They are keenly interested in the very early precursors of anti-social, as well as pro-social, behavior. When we understand what might be harbingers of serious problems much later on, then we can determine possible ways to intervene.

The role of parents in monitoring, supervising and guiding their children through the turbulent years of adolescence is more critical than ever. When parents "bail out" too soon, because of their child's need for autonomy or because they feel criticized or pushed away, they are likely to miss signs of trouble. It is one thing for a teenager to want his privacy. It is another for him to isolate himself in his room from the moment he gets home until late at night, playing video games that provide practice in killing others.

"Who are your friends and how do you spend your time?" is not a question we can afford to stop asking when they turn 13. Also, looks can be deceiving. What may be a harmless clothing fad could also be a "look" that alienates them socially or aligns them with gangs.

Last, not every teen who is feeling the pain of a relationship breaking up becomes despondent or suicidal or homicidal. But, if parents minimize the loss of a relationship as "puppy love," they may also miss signs of serious trouble. The end of love at this age ranges from relief to emotional devastation. We cannot assume that "they will get over it" because they are young and there are "lots of fish in the sea." We must be vigilant, supportive, and willing to intervene, even if our intervention is unwelcome.

The Littleton school massacre intensified a debate over whether the entertainment industry has helped create what some call a culture of violence. Morbid computer games, music about death and drugs, and movies about kids who solve their problems with cruel mind games and murder are being scrutinized.

A May 1999, USA Today/CNN/Gallup poll showed 49 percent of respondents believe that the popular media, including movies, television and music, had a "great deal" of blame for the Colorado shootings. (A larger percentage of respondents, however, placed blame on parents and the availability of guns.)

Fifty-two percent said they consider restrictions on television and movie violence as "very effective" means to help stop school violence.

Steve Rickard, an officer with the Denver Police Department's gang unit, said emotional problems with roots in the home life—and not entertainment—appear to have the biggest influence on why children turn to gangs and violence. He found many youths go to gangs or cults seeking acceptance, a feeling of self worth and a sense of identity.

But he added: "A lot of times entertainment—music, movies—is the trigger. It's not the cause, necessarily, it's the little push that makes them do something."

On May 20, 1999, the Senate passed a landmark bill that imposed tough gun control measures. It would require strict background checks on all firearm transactions at gun shows and pawn shops. It limits sales of assault weapons to minors, bans the import of high-capacity magazines, and denies juveniles convicted of a felony the right to purchase a gun for life. The legislation would also make it a crime to distribute bomb-making information for criminal purposes.

The bill was viewed by many as an expression of Middle America's anxiety over school violence. Efforts to pass this bill galvanized in the weeks following the Littleton tragedy, and within hours of a shooting at one of the highest ranking schools in the nation, Heritage High in Conyers, Georgia, where a 15-year-old teen wounded six people.

Proposed legislative action like this signals a shift in our thinking as a country and a commitment to protect children, in the face of out-of-control weapons abuse. But, as with all emotionally-driven efforts, there is the risk that loopholes and short-sightedness may flaw a law's original intent.

Three Strikes Law Strikes Out?

Consider the "three strikes" law in California. Designed to imprison repeat felons, it was pushed by a public and political groundswell following the kidnapping and murder of 12-year old Polly Klaas in 1993. It is the most stringent mandatory sentencing law in the in the United Sates. Even before it was in effect, some envisioned the initiative as unfairly targeting the repeat offenders whose crimes were not violent.

In retrospect, they seem to have been correct. 80% of offenders sentenced under the "three strikes" law committed non-violent crimes.

The ramifications include costly expansion of the prison system at the expense of other state needs, such as education. Add to that the frustration of court officials, who are no longer allowed to use discretion in sentencing repeat offenders, even when cases involve drugs, grand theft or burglary, all considered nonviolent.

Some argue that because crime rates have gone down, the law is doing its job. How can we afford to change the law to only apply to violent crimes, when the statistics show significant improvement? Obviously, this is not an easy question to answer and will be debated again.

Controversy Around Chemical Castration

We are a nation struggling to find the right answers. On September 17, 1996 California became the first state in the nation to chemically castrate twice-convicted child molesters under a bill signed by then Governor Pete Wilson.

Under the bill, twice-convicted molesters would receive injections of Depo-Provera shortly before being released from prison. The shots would continue until a panel of experts deem the molester to be rehabilitated or until the parole period ends.

The law lets convicted offenders choose between temporary chemical castration or permanent castration by surgical removal of the testicles.

The American Civil Liberties Union oppose this action, contending that castration is "cruel and unusual" punishment and may violate a person's right to privacy.

Medical experts remain divided over the effectiveness of chemical castration in preventing sex offenses. Some question its effectiveness without therapy, which is not provided for or required in the bill.

Others argue that recidivism rates of molesters in countries using chemical or surgical castration have dropped. According to supporters, Norway, Switzerland, Denmark and Sweden surgically or chemically castrate sex offenders and have seen the rate of repeat sexual offenses decline sharply, from nearly 100 percent to just 2 percent.

Those who advocate treatment, but not castration, believe it is a myth that sexual molestation is a habit that is impossible to break. According to the Association for the Treatment of Sexual Abusers, the re-offense rate for untreated sex offenders who primarily target children ranges in various studies from 10 percent to 40 percent, not the "80 percent to 90 percent" that many lay people conclude after watching the 6 o'clock news.

They claim that experts can predict which offenders are most likely to get into trouble again and that at least some sex offenders can be treated. They also agree that sadists and killers, such as Richard Allen Davis, who murdered Polly Klaas, are not going to respond to treatment and are too dangerous to let out.

An important goal of treatment is to instill victim empathy and to get the perpetrator to appreciate the consequences of his acts to his family, his friends, and himself. Acknowledging the futility of knowing why someone is aroused by exposing himself to children, the therapists who treat pedophiles encourage them to control the impulse, to modify their fantasies and, at all costs, to stay out of playgrounds.

A 1993 study led by R. Karl Hanson of the Canadian Solicitor General's office found that about 42% of imprisoned child molesters are later re-convicted for violent or sexual crimes—whether they received therapy or not. In addition, therapy programs generally only accept "treatable" criminals, such as non-violent pedophiles, shunning serial rapists and violent offenders.

So, is rehabilitation possible? Pedophiles are among the most difficult sex offenders to treat. Short-term intensive rehabilitation can stop pedophiles for a while, but most experts agree that a significant number will molest again after three or four years.

I happen to believe that pedophilia is an addiction. As in other forms of addiction, some addicts are amenable to treatment and some are not. Effective rehabilitation would combine several methods: one-on-one counseling, chemical castration to lower sex drive, group therapy, and twelve-step programs similar to those used to treat alcoholism and drug addiction. If treatment is not warranted, I support the next option.

Extending Sexual Predators' Stay

In 1996, Kansas became the first state to require some violent sexual predators to remain in custody for years beyond their sentence. Other states like California followed suit. After scores of defendants throughout the state challenged the law, the state appeals court ruled that it is constitutional to allow serial rapists and child molesters to be locked up indefinitely, even though they have finished their prison sentences.

The sexual predator law allows individuals, who have been convicted of violent sex crimes against two or more people and are judged likely to continue committing such crimes, to be confined to the locked ward of a mental hospital until they are deemed no longer a threat to others.

Supporters of the law insist that society must be protected from violent sexual offenders who cannot or will not change their ways. They also contend that commitment to a mental institution is not a new criminal punishment but necessary psychological treatment.

The law imposes a mental health commitment for a *present* diagnosed mental illness which makes it likely the predator will commit *future* sexually violent offenses. The sexual predator law remains one of the most volatile criminal issues in the nation, pitting supporters against civil libertarians who believe it violates due process and the Constitution's protection against double jeopardy.

Megan's Law: The Most Controversial of All

Megan Kanka, 7, was raped and murdered July 1994 in Hamilton Township, New Jersey, by a twice convicted sex offender, who lived across the street. Her parents lobbied for laws giving the public more information about the identities and whereabouts of known sex offenders.

In May 1996, President Clinton signed a law that requires all states to provide the public with information about sex offenders.

The bill has three parts:

1. Police may notify individuals or affected community groups that a sex offender lives nearby.
2. Police may advertise to the entire community, in any way they determine appropriate, the presence of high-risk registered sex offenders.

3. The public can visit sheriff's offices or big-city police departments and look at a CD-ROM containing data.

Megan's Law is controversial. Civil libertarians say it tramples on the constitutional rights of ex-convicts who already have paid their debt to society. Critics say it spurs vigilantism, drives sex offenders away from treatment, and does not necessarily reduce crime.

Let's look at how citizens, courts, law enforcement agencies, and even business have interpreted the law over the past few years.

In August 1997, the Third U.S. Circuit Court of Appeals in Philadelphia upheld New Jersey Megan's Law. It rejected a challenge from public defenders who had contended that the New Jersey law was unconstitutional because it inflicted extra "punishment" on paroled sex offenders after they had served jail time for their offenses.

In a split ruling, a three-judge panel concluded that dissemination of information about paroled sex offenders was not punitive and did not violate the U.S. Constitution.

"Registration and carefully tailored notification can enable law enforcement officials and those likely to encounter a sex offender to be aware of a potential danger and to stay vigilant against possible re-abuse," the court's decision said.

It was the highest federal court to rule on the constitutionality of community-notification laws, enacted in recent years by nearly every state in the nation.

Eighteen months later, 700 Santa Rosa, California residents were warned about six convicted sex offenders who police believed pose a continuing threat to women and children in the area. In addition to residents, the flyers went to school districts, libraries, businesses, and possibly shopping centers.

Chief Olivares said his department waited about a year to start the door-to-door campaign because officials wanted to determine whether lawsuits would overturn Megan's Law.

Just days after Santa Rosa police went door to door to warn

his neighbors that he was a convicted rapist and child molester, Michael Allen Patton, a registered sex offender, was found hanged. Patton left a suicide note. He was one of six high-risk predators Santa Rosa police officers named.

Police Chief Michael Dunbaugh said Patton's apparent suicide would have no effect on the police department's policy of notifying neighbors about potential sexual predators.

When residents in Dilley, Oregon learned that a child molester was about to move in, they talked of getting guard dogs, arming themselves, burning down his home, even killing him. In the end, they did something more peaceful: they bought the house out from under him.

Child abuse experts and law enforcement officials said this was the first time a community tried to block a molester from moving in by buying him out.

While the parole officer said the house appeared to meet basic surveillance requirements for freed sex offenders because it sat isolated from children in the middle of 27 acres of pasture, the neighbors disagreed. They mobilized when they realized the site—nestled in chest-high grass miles away from the nearest police station—provided perfect cover for a sexual predator.

Critics of Megan's law say it falls short because it only pertains to sex offenders who have been in prison. The majority of sex offenders have only been sentenced to county jail time. They argue that there could be many victims before someone draws a prison sentence.

There continues to be a need for greater cooperation between jurisdictions and more vigilance in checking criminal histories once a suspect is in custody. In addition, some advocate reclassifying what we now view as minor offenses—like peeking in windows—even though no major criminal offense has yet occurred. We need also to consider the underlying reasons for some of these behavioral offenses.

I remember a book written by a serial rapist who scoffed at the law enforcement officials who had arrested him nine times for window peeking, and then let him go, while the majority of their department's efforts were spent on finding the rapist. He was the rapist. "How do they think I picked my victims?" he asked.

Registries Are Popular

Virginia is the latest state to put the names and addresses of its convicted sex offenders on the Internet. Nine others, plus several individual counties and cities, have already done it. In states such as California, which don't post the official registry online, private citizens often create Web sites and publish their own sketchy lists.

These registries, which often include the exact address, place of employment and even photos of convicted sex offenders, have become popular. Alaska's site recorded more than 73,000 hits in its first year. In Bellingham, Washington, nearly 18,000 people—equivalent to a third of the population—had visited the city's online registry, which lists six men.

In June 1997, California became the first state in the nation to use a computer CD-ROM to give public access to the names of nearly every sex offender in any community.

Soon after, a tiny rural newspaper became the first in California to print the names of every serious sex offender in its county. The decision drew harsh criticism and a death threat to the paper's editor. It is the only instance of a community's entire Megan's Law CD-ROM log going to press. The editor said he got unhappy calls from people who were either on the list or had a relative on it. But then he got "40 calls from people who were all for it."

From the start, civil libertarians were alarmed at the possibility of the lists being used to instigate vigilantism. "The main problem with this kind of listing is that it is another means of subtly encouraging vigilantism," said Elizabeth Schroeder, an associate director for the state ACLU.

The zeal with which some of these registries are publicized sits uncomfortably with me. It's unfair that a person who has paid a debt to society is tainted forever for his or her crime.

But, I also can't help thinking that since the child will be paying for the molester's crime for the rest of his or her life, why shouldn't the molester?

Social issues are so cleanly and smartly debated across a lawyer's conference table. But watch a chubby pair of legs toddling toward the door, and idealism steps aside to protect children, at almost any cost.

The general sentiment around Megan's Law seems to be: "I know there's controversy, but it's for the greater good."

Are We Scaring Away the Wrong People?

A lunchtime playground supervisor at an elementary school quit her job after the principal ordered her to stop hugging students.

Donna Jones said children need hugs, and she cannot abide by the embracing embargo declared at Schafer Park Elementary School by Principal Jim Hough. "I told him, 'You have allowed these kids to hug me for the last three years and they trust me. I cannot stop that,'" Jones said.

Hough asked Jones to stop hugging children after two parents raised objections. One of the parents said she is not worried that Jones is touching her children improperly, but said her kids were uncomfortable with the attention.

"Taking their concerns into consideration, as well as the job responsibilities of the noontime supervisor, I instructed people not to hug the children," Hough said.

For three consecutive summers, I provided in-service training to the youth counselors at a community center day camp. It was a joy to see these young people so excited about the prospect of working with kids for the summer. The first time I looked out at their fresh, clean-cut faces, I thought, "Is this training really necessary?" Nevertheless, I proceeded to present information and lead discussions about how touching, hugging, and other affectionate gestures might be misconstrued by some children or their parents.

I demonstrated the subtle difference between displaying warmth and encouragement and getting too close. We practiced showing each other physical affection and noting at which point we began to stiffen or pull away, or became passive, all nonverbal signs that we were not enjoying the physical contact. I encouraged them to be alert to those possible reactions from their campers and to back off if a child showed any hint of discomfort. By the way, during my three years of serving as a consultant to the camp, I had to report two incidents of suspected sexual misconduct. Yes, I do believe the training is necessary.

Showing appropriate affection is a very "touchy" matter because children vary so much in how they like to receive attention. Some are so hungry for physical closeness they would sit in our laps all day if we allowed them to. Others, who may be more self-contained or a little shy, appreciate an encouraging word or a smile, but shrink from a friendly hug. The two main points I emphasize with all professionals and volunteers who work with children are these: (1) our best defense against accusations of sexual misconduct is to understand and honor the physical boundaries each individual child needs, and (2) each adult working with children should have some alternative ways of showing affection that don't involve physically touching children. In chapter 3, I'll give you some positive and creative ways to praise children that you can add to your own repertoire.

Today's teachers are sensitive to this issue of misconduct, as allegations ring out from classrooms around the country. Male teachers, particularly, are worried that casual physical contact with children may create the impression of sexual misconduct. What adds to their dilemma is the pressure they feel to be more caring and demonstrative to children. It would be a shame to close the door on appropriate roles for caring men, to discourage them from being warm and comforting to children because of some misplaced belief that they are suspect if they get physically close.

In preschools and day-care centers, male teachers tell me that now they don't change children's wet clothing—at least not without a female teacher standing by to observe. They used to tickle kids. Now they don't for fear that bystanders will question their motives. Some kids who want and expect hugs from their teachers will go without them now. The safeguards that are in place to protect all our children are not perfect, but unfortunately they are necessary. This is the price all of our teachers—and children—must pay for the behavior of a few.

Internet Pedophiles Exceed All Predictions

In 1994, when I wrote the first edition of this book, law enforcement agencies and on-line services companies were just beginning to realize that pedophilia and pornographers were benefiting from the Internet. It became alarmingly clear that the Internet had become a playground for perverts, providing them with a cloak of anonymity under which to operate more effectively.

Detectives throughout the country now see the need to focus on the Internet, where millions of young computer users are at risk of being seduced by sexual predators each day. In addition, the Child Online Protection Act now makes it a crime to make certain types of graphic sexual material available to children younger than 17 years old.

San Jose's child exploitation detail, the first of its kind in California, has cracked cases nation-wide by posing undercover online. The Sexual Assault Felony Enforcement team, made up of officers from local, state, and federal agencies, also infiltrates the Web to catch pedophiles.

Most free-speech advocates don't object to police posing undercover on the Internet. But they say that there is nothing illegal about people merely discussing their desire to perform acts that might be illegal.

However, if those interests extend to sexually explicit pictures being passed from friend to friend, it is a felony, according to the law. For example, in the Wonderland Club, prospective members were required to supply 10,000 images of kiddie porn to join, authorities said.

Even more chilling, according to investigators, is the international network of pedophiles who use the Internet to trade sexually explicit photographs of minors and participate in interactive online child molestations using digital cameras.

According to prosecutors, members of the notorious Orchid Club molested a 10-year-old girl, while members all over the world watched and participated by asking for various poses via the Internet. One man who took part from Illinois admitted to FBI agents that he joined the group because he thought the Internet was safe—far away from the probing eyes of law enforcement.

The group, which met in an Internet chat room, swapped stories about child sex and exchanged sexually explicit pictures of young girls. Ringleaders of the child-pornography operation were sent to federal prison, following their 1996 conviction. And investigators now use seized pictures to solve missing-children cases.

Precise numbers are difficult to come by, but more and more pedophiles from around the globe are using the World Wide Web to prey on young, unsuspecting victims, investigators say. They troll chat rooms looking for naïve victims and use the Internet to exchange child pornography internationally.

"I hope this doesn't add to the general misperception that online is riddled with pornography and that a child is unsafe online," said Elizabeth Lipson, an online veteran and commentator. "They are as safe online as any playground a parent checks out ahead of time." What Ms. Lipson fails to consider is that while we can see what kind of adults are at a playground, we can't see what kind of adults are online.

On the Internet, as in any community, most of the people are wonderful most of the time. But the Internet also has its organized racist groups, its perverts and just plain bad people.

An Inside Job

On February 5, 1997 authorities revealed the existence of a list of 5,000 to 6,000 children's names found on a computer used by George Chamberlain, an inmate at Lino Lakes prison. The names on the first list were mostly children living in outstate Minnesota.

The FBI later informed the Department of Corrections of a second list of around 2,600 names, mostly from the Minneapolis-St.Paul area. Corrections officials began mailing out letters the next day to parents whose children's names appear on the list.

The list appeared to have been assembled from 1987 to 1993, using mostly information from local newspapers, newscasts, and high school yearbooks. Prisoners obtained newspapers from all over the state through a newspaper exchange.

The computers was one of several owned by a private tele-marketing company that employed prisoners to help the inmate raise money for their educations. Computers were confiscated in 1994 when an investigation by a local TV station alleged that prisoners were engaging in profitable activities on the side, unbeknownst to prison officials.

Since the investigation, the modems have been removed and inmates are no longer able to connect to the Internet. "There was no evidence to suggest the list was distributed over the Internet or by any other means," said Dennis Benson, Deputy Commissioner of Corrections. "This is an embarrassing situation for the department. But this is also a wakeup call for parents. This is not unique to prisons. It can be occurring anywhere."

So, what will help us protect children who "surf the net?"

- **Parental supervision** of home computers to make sure their children are not lured into interaction with potentially dangerous strangers.
- **Software** that blocks inappropriate material for young users

- **On-line service monitors** watching for abuses
- **Closing accounts** of subscribers who repeatedly violate rules
- Distributing **child safety brochures** to parents
- Teaching safety skills to children

There are hundreds of Internet sites offering advice on how to protect you and child online. Among them are:

- http://www.yahooligans.com/docs/safety
- http://www.cyberangels.org/chatsmarts.html
- http://www.cyberangels.org/AOLsmarts.html
- http://www.nvc.org/ddir/info44.htm

The FBI offers a free brochure, *A Parents' Guide to Internet Safety.* Download it from the FBI's Web site (www.fbi.gov) or contact your nearest FBI office and request a copy from the Crimes Against Children Coordinator.

The National Center for Missing and Exploited Children offers two free brochures: *Child Safety on the Information Highway* and *Teen Safety on the Information Highway.* To order, write National Center for Missing and Exploited Children, 2101 Wilson Blvd., Department P, Suite 550, Arlington, VA 22201-30777 or visit www.missingkids.com on the Web.

Where Do We Go From Here?

I agree with Andrew Vachss, child advocate, who recommends that radical changes be made to our criminal justice system, in order to protect our children from predators—online and off. Write to your legislators, talk to you law-enforcement agencies and organize a community campaign to get these changes made.

Some of Vachss recommendations that I support:

1. The FBI's National Sex Offender Registry, a computerized database of convicted pedophile that is slated to be operat-

ing by summer 1999. It makes background checks almost instantaneously available to law-enforcement agencies. This means that any organization allowing a person on the registry to have access to children should be held accountable if a child is harmed. No excuses. State participation in the registry is voluntary, however. If your state is not taking part, urge your legislators to take action.

2. Increase the penalties for all "enticement" crimes aimed at children, including attempts. Such penalties should be enhanced when the perpetrator had prior convictions, used "camouflage" (as in chat room) or abused a position of trust, (such as teacher, counselor, or coach).

3. Change the labeling of predatory behavior. The criminal justice system characterized the enticement of children for sexual abuse—indeed, any sexual abuse short of forcible rape—as a "nonviolent" crime. More often than not, these crimes have a horribly violent , traumatic effect, whether the predator was "violent" or not.

4. The law must impose liability on organizations, agencies and institutions that negligently expose children to predators. This should include the public, private volunteer and religious sectors. That liability must be expanded to include instances when pedophiles are "recycled" after agreeing to treatment and put back into positions of trust. If an organization decides such an individual is "cured" and returns him to a different program or community without disclosing his prior history to the parents, that organization., should be held accountable for any harm which results. Given the rates of recidivism, and the number of children predators harm over a lifetime, we must carefully consider if and when to let them rejoin our communities.

5. Empty the prisons of genuinely nonviolent offenders and fill the vacancies with child-sex predators. These predators have, up to now, enjoyed probation and short sentences. Once we have them where they belong, we must keep them there longer.

CHAPTER 3

Turning Nice Kids into Safe Kids

Sweet, polite kids are not safe kids. All children are vulnerable to crime, but children who are too obedient are more likely to become victimized by sex offenders. Children who are taught that assertive behavior is disrespectful don't develop the skills to safely respond to would-be abusers.

According to psychologist and child development expert Penelope Leach, we must try not to discipline our children in a way that assumes they should do only as they are told—whatever they are told. Nor should they have to obey grown-ups just because they are adults. She emphasizes that if children are going to learn to protect themselves from misused power, they have to be empowered to question orders they do not understand and to refuse orders that feel wrong.

Children who feel unloved or lonely are more at risk. We know that child molesters seek out children in need of love or affection because they are easy targets. Sex offenders and kidnappers target kids who look vulnerable, who seem sad or lonely, who they know have trouble in their lives, and who don't feel good about themselves. In studying victims of sexual abuse, we've learned that when children are starved for affection, they are more likely to rationalize the molester's suspicious or confusing behavior. Many pedophiles and child pornographers successfully take advantage of many different victims because they invest time and effort to win children's confidence. They become a child's best buddy, someone who "really understands" her problems. Sometimes the hugs and kisses of an abuser are welcomed by affection-hungry children, tolerated as just one more odd behavior in an adult repertoire that is often incomprehensible, or regarded as a fair price for candy and treats.

Molesters have figured out which qualities to look for in their victims: naïveté, natural curiosity, a need to be loved, and the ability and willingness to keep a secret. For a child, the secrecy attached to the relationship can be part of the fun: a private one-upmanship over parents who are less flattering than the abuser, brothers and sisters who do not get to share these candies, or classmates who have not been singled out because they aren't as "special."

Everything we've learned from children who have been victimized has taught us how sex offenders think and act: They are highly strategic and are notoriously personable with children. Two things have become very clear. Our best prevention of abuse is to promote self-esteem in children from early on, and we need to establish open communication within the family. How to do that is the focus of this chapter.

Finding the Words and the Way

Remember some of the secrets you kept as a child? Some you kept because you didn't want to be punished; some you decided not to tell because you didn't want your parents to be disappointed in you. But how about the secrets you kept because you felt ashamed or confused? How about the secrets that seemed unspeakable?

In the news this past year was the story of a ten-year-old girl who, sensing that her cousin was being coaxed away by a child molester, charged into the man's house and rescued her. The girl's instincts were right, and her brave action prevented her cousin from being victimized. Three months later, the same man attempted to entice another child and was arrested. What struck me about this incident—aside from the girl's courage—was the fact that she had kept it a total secret for three months. It was only when she overheard her mother discussing the news report and the crime was out in the open that she came forward with her own account. In a television interview, she was asked why she hadn't told her mother sooner. Her answer still haunts me. She said, "I didn't know what to say."

This incident illustrates the important truth about how children perceive what's OK or not OK to talk about. Children don't automatically know how to talk about difficult things. They need us to give them the *words* and the *way*. When sexual abuse and other sensitive subjects are not discussed in the home, children are likely to infer that such matters are unspeakable.

In every family there are implicit understandings—unspoken rules about what may and may not be discussed. These "rules" dictate how much openness there is, and function as a sort of code about what topics are off-limits. I've noticed in working with families that although no one says a word, it's very clear when we've ventured into topics that are "just not discussed." Often there is an incident or event families prefer to keep hidden and not to discuss. Inevitably, I discover that although a particular event has never been discussed aloud, each family member—even the littlest one—knows what it is and thinks about it. And sometimes it's not the topic that is taboo; rather, it's certain emotions—hatred, envy, sadness—that are not allowed. When families are emotionally constricted, children have a harder time feeling safe and secure and are less likely to share their troubles with their parents.

Every family has its dangerous or embarrassing or shameful or guilty secrets, its unspeakable stories: a crime, a child born out of wedlock, a drinking problem, a secret marriage. While parents often hope to save themselves and their children by avoiding talking about an upsetting change or a disturbing event in their lives, kids find things out—particularly hidden things, things parents don't want to talk about. The problem with "shielding" children from traumatic events by not address-ing them directly is that children's imaginations can—and do—run wild.

I remember a ten-year-old girl whose parents were trying to shield her from some financial problems the family was having. Almost every night, the stress and conflict between her parents erupted in loud verbal arguments. These arguments were unusual for the couple, and the daughter became very worried. Her only experience with this kind of angry shouting was on television. Unfortunately, in all the TV shows she had watched, people fought like this just before somebody got killed, so she became very frightened whenever she heard her parents argue. When the girl's parents were made aware of how their wish to protect their daughter had backfired, they explained what they were worried about—in simple and reassuring terms—and the girl stopped imagining the worst.

Some parents say that they do not want to darken their child's early life by talking about unpleasant subjects like sexual abuse. Unfortunately, this may mean that the only information that the child gets about sexual abuse is from a sexual abuser. The child concludes that since Mom and Dad don't talk about this, it *must* be bad. Therefore, he can't talk to his parents about it or they will be mad at him.

This is exactly what molesters are counting on—that the child has not been given any information about sexual abuse, and that he won't tell his parents. Furthermore, molesters rely on the fact that children will feel an obligation to them because of the attention and gifts they have given to them. What often permanently silences children is that once the friendship is established, the abuser uses scare tactics to blackmail or frighten the child into not telling her parents. Strategically placing each emotional brick, the molester builds a wall between the child and her family—with gifts and attention, guilt, and, finally, threats of harm—to cut the child off from people who can help. Once a wall of secrecy and fear is built, the child can be easily manipulated into granting sexual favors.

Since children have no previous experience with sex or sexual abuse, they need accurate, healthy information from parents. If we aren't discussing these subjects, we are isolating our children and making them too vulnerable to learning about "appropriate" sexual contact from the wrong person.

Walking Your Talk

No matter what we say or how open we seem, it's what our children *observe* that ultimately determines how much they are willing to share with us. Children pick up cues about what's safe to discuss and what's unsafe to bring up. For example, if children risk vulnerable, intimate feelings and are met with harsh criticism, they quickly learn to keep such feelings to themselves. If a parent becomes overwhelmed at the first mention of unpleasantness, the child starts to keep his troubles to himself. Or, if a parent typically overreacts or moves into action without regard to the child's needs or wishes, the child learns not to share because his parents "always make too big a deal out of it."

Sometimes adults cut off communication to protect themselves from hearing the disturbing truth. The parent who denies or obliterates the clues she gets from her child about incest or sexual abuse is a classic example. Sometimes parents even go so far as to punish the child for revealing the incest or blame the child for making it happen. Assurances like "you know you can talk about anything with me" mean very little if the adults in the child's life don't listen and respond sensitively. For those children who conclude that confusing, disturbing issues can't be discussed, growing up can be a lonely and scary journey.

Whether or not your child will come to you with problems really depends on your day-to-day communications and how you listen during normal conversations. Let's face it, sometimes it's hard to keep listening to a three-year-old's stream of talk, but there are often important messages in their "baby talk." Try not to switch over to automatic pilot and respond with unthinking "reallys?" and "uh-huhs."

Kids do notice if you're listening to them, and if they are tuned out time and time again, there are serious consequences. Toddlers who are ignored, for example, grow into small children who don't make much of an effort to communicate with others. Preschoolers who feel unheard act out their anger and frustration. Often we mistake this for "naughty behavior."

Another way a child can feel unheard is when you dismiss his common childhood fears like being afraid of the dark or of being separated from you. If you dismiss such fears, how can he assume that you'll take him seriously if he tells you about a person who frightens him in some way he cannot quite describe?

Kids are resilient. They give us hundreds of chances to get it right. Nevertheless, your child will not confide in you if she frequently dislikes the results. If you encourage your child to own up to wrongdoings and then get angry or punish her, she may decide that she would rather risk being found out than coming forward to face your wrath. Ideally, you want your child to know that if she comes forward there is nothing to fear, that whatever the problem is, you will work it out together.

Who Listened to You?

Many of us had upsetting sexual experiences as children: a man exposed himself to us on the playground, a family friend gave us a drunken kiss, a stranger rubbed against us in a crowded elevator, a baby-sitter showed us "what married people do," a minister hugged us too long and too intimately, a neighbor invited us over for a "special game" in the garage. Such memories stay with us into our adulthood. Many of these memories remain secrets.

Several years ago, a woman came to see me, suddenly flooded with vivid memories of sexual abuse. She recalled with horror that from the time she was five until she was eleven, her father had used her to satisfy his sexual needs. When her daughter turned five, she started feeling tremendous anxiety for reasons she didn't understand. She had become extremely worried that her husband was seducing her daughter. As her worry increased, so did the explicit memories she had blotted out for twenty-five years.

Why did she keep such horrible abuse a secret? For one thing, she felt powerless about exposing her father; she thought no one would believe her claims about such a respected and powerful man. For another, her father, a masterful manipulator, had convinced her that she was to blame. With her sense of right and wrong so twisted, with her need to trust her father and depend on him so exploited, she did what many victims of child abuse do in order to survive. She pretended the incest didn't happen.

If you were sexually abused and you never told anyone, you may have kept it a secret out of shame or confusion. Or, maybe you wanted to tell, but you felt that no one would listen to you or believe you. If this was the case, then you know firsthand what it feels like to go unheard, to bear a terrible burden silently and alone.

Recently, a thirteen-year-old girl wrote to "Dear Abby," troubled by an incident that had occurred with her sister's husband when he drove her to pick up her bike at a friend's house after dark. Earlier that day, her brother-in-law had told her how beautiful she was and that he'd been noticing how well she was developing. Driving home, he suddenly stopped the truck and asked for a hug. The girl thought, "What the heck, he did me a favor to drive me to pick up my bike, so it's no big deal to give him a hug." But it went on too long, and he wouldn't let her go; then he wanted a kiss. The girl was only able to stop him by shouting "NO!" repeatedly. She wrote to Dear Abby because now she felt terribly uncomfortable around him. What struck me was her comment: "I can't tell my sister or anyone else because my sister really loves him and I couldn't live with myself if I made trouble in her marriage."

Obviously, this young woman needed to tell someone, or she wouldn't have written to Dear Abby. Her feelings of being alone with this secret were causing her pain. Abby thanked her for warning other young girls who could be taken advantage of by a relative or a close friend. What wasn't said, however, was that this girl needs help in stopping her brother-in-law's inappropriate sexual overtures. Not only that, based on what is known about molesters it is naive to assume that this was the first time he had approached a minor. It's also possible that one of the reasons she's not speaking up is that she feels guilty about having enjoyed her brother-in-law's attention. And she may feel foolish because she didn't anticipate what would follow when he complimented her about her body earlier that day.

When a teenager's already conflicted feelings become so entangled, it takes a nonjudgmental adult to listen objectively and help sort them out. And if that person can't be a family member, then telling another trusted adult is crucial. The girl needs to be educated that even though she is not without sexual charms, her sister's husband chose her because *he was certain she wouldn't tell.* She must tell her family what happened, maybe with the help of another adult, so that her brother-in-law's inappropriate behavior stops once and for all.

Listening on Purpose

None of us wants our children to feel that they can't come to us, yet there are times in our day-to-day conversations with our kids that we send mixed messages about being there for them. For example, we've all had the experience of half-listening to our children when we're distracted, busy, or uninterested. Chances are your child got frustrated and said, "You're not listening!" Or maybe he didn't protest but simply gave up and walked away. The fact is, when we're distracted we're not listening to our kids effectively. We miss information and, even though we want to believe otherwise, our children pick up that we're only half there.

Have you ever told your child, "I can read the newspaper *and* listen to you" or "Not now! I'm on the phone!"? It's better to listen with your eyes *and* your ears, to listen to and watch what your children are saying, so that you can pick up the important messages that are often hidden just below the surface. And, if you can't stop what you're doing right then, be sure to let your child know you'll make time to talk later.

Often children signal their feelings to you with their body language. For example, you might notice that your child is avoiding eye contact—a clue that what he is trying to tell you is hard to talk about. Or maybe his eye twitches or his lip trembles—a sign that intense feelings are building up. Sometimes kids hang their heads or slump their shoulders—an indication that they're feeling weighted down with worry or sadness.

Listen on two levels: listen to what they say and what they *don't* say. If the way your child looks and behaves communicates something very different from what her words are telling you, trust your instincts. Only by watching and noticing can you pick up these important clues.

Here are six things you can do to show your children that you're ready to listen and hear what they have to say. These six techniques help to build trust and enable you to be alert to and aware of any potential problems:

1. Eliminate distractions.
2. Turn toward your child.
3. Keep eye contact.
4. Express a caring attitude in your face and voice.
5. Be an active listener. Say "Oh," "I see," and "Mmm . . . " to acknowledge what is being said and to encourage her to keep sharing her thoughts and feelings.
6. Give your child's feeling a name.

I'm going to focus on the sixth technique because parents most often ask me for help with this one. Have you ever poured your heart out to a friend who, when you were finished, said *exactly* what you needed to hear? There's nothing like feeling understood when you are sharing your feelings with another person. Nothing builds trust and intimacy more than knowing that when you risk your innermost feelings and thoughts, the person you're telling will respond with complete understanding. I've met many people in my life who have never had this experience, who think that being able to guess exactly how another person is feeling is nothing short of magic. Well, it's not magic. It's recognizing certain emotions when you see or hear them. It's learning how to name them and reflect them back to the person who is speaking.

Some parents ask me, "What if I don't guess the right feeling?" It's been my experience in working with children that if the child senses that you are trying to understand, she'll give you the benefit of the doubt. And often, if you don't name their feelings correctly, children will come back and name them for you! "I'm not *mad* about this, Mom! I'm *hurt*!" Don't take this kind of feedback personally. It's just part of your ongoing training as a good listener.

What children don't easily forget, however, is when you miss the point of what they're trying to tell you altogether. Sometimes listening for hidden feelings instead of taking your child's words at face value is the best way to avoid this problem. And don't be afraid to ask for more information if you don't understand.

Here's what happens when a mother can't comprehend what her eleven-year-old son is trying to tell her:

Alex: I don't want to walk to school anymore with Bill and Joe. They're weirdos!
Mom: I know that their families aren't as fortunate as ours, but that's no reason to refuse to walk with them.
Alex: Oh, Mom, that's not what I mean!

Compare the interaction above with the one that follows. This time the mother listens for the feelings behind the words:

Alex: I don't want to walk to school anymore with Bill and Joe. They're weirdos!
Mom: It sounds like you're upset with the way the boys are behaving. What's up?

Alex: Well, it's kind of embarrassing. . . . Every time we go down the path behind the school, they try to pull down my jeans and mess with me. They won't stop!

Mom: Well, no wonder you don't want to walk with them! They're not behaving the way friends should. I'm glad you came to me. I know it wasn't easy. Now we can find a solution together.

Here are some more examples where the parent comprehends what the child is saying and then responds in an open and compassionate way:

Child: John called me a baby because I wouldn't cut across the parking lot on my way home!

Parent: It must have hurt when John called you a baby, especially when he's such a good friend of yours.

Child: Uncle Herb wouldn't stop tickling me when I told him to stop. He wouldn't listen even though I said it over and over again!

Parent: I can see why you're feeling so angry and frustrated. It's disappointing when someone you love takes advantage of you. Do you need my help in talking to Uncle Herb about this?

Child: Mom, I'd feel like an idiot shouting "Stop! Leave me alone! I don't know you!" Everyone would stare at me.

Parent: You're right. You might feel embarrassed because you're not used to drawing that kind of attention to yourself. But this technique will get people to help you in an emergency, so you've got to be willing to make a scene if you're in trouble.

Notice in the second and third examples that while the adults empathized with the children and accepted their feelings, they did not back down or change the rule or behavior that needed to be enforced. In the case of the tickling uncle, notice how sensitive the parent was in asking the child if she needed help. This kind of offer would reassure rather than alarm a child, because the parent involves the child in choosing how they will resolve the problem. Whether or not the issue will be addressed is *not* the child's choice; however, *how* to approach Uncle Herb is.

In every case, the adults took a "guess" at what the children were feeling when they responded. They used feeling words like *angry, frustrated, hurt,* and *embarrassed.* There are hundreds of feeling words, but here are some of the basic ones, in no particular order:

sad	embarrassed	excited	angry	guilty
happy	lonely	worried	frightened	ashamed
mad	upset	loving	scared	disappointed
jealous	confused	close	confident	afraid
hurt	unhappy	unsure	brave	proud

Have you ever been criticized or punished for expressing any of the feelings on this list? As you read through this list, are there any feelings you think are wrong to have? If expressing certain feelings had negative consequences for you as a child, you'll need to work hard to accept and understand those same feelings in your children. Sometimes it helps to remember what you wished someone had said to you when you were having those feelings. It may feel new and strange to say something accepting and supportive to your kids when they share their feelings. But wait until you see the look in their eyes when they feel you really understand! It's worth it.

Now imagine your response to this child's statement:

Child: I don't like always having to play with someone else when I'm in my own yard! You don't trust me! You treat me like a baby!

Your response: _____

_____

_____

Possible response: I understand that you don't want to feel like a baby and I'm sorry this rule makes you feel like one. I wish all of our safety rules could feel fair to you. Now, either I can sit on the steps while you play or you can invite a friend over. You choose.

The key here is to name the feeling, empathize with the child, and then simply restate the limit. You're not, after all, going to change the rule because he doesn't like it. But you can express your regret that this rule makes him feel uncomfortable or unhappy.

If you had trouble with this exercise, start observing your child's feelings during the day and taking some verbal guesses. Be sure to name the positive feelings you observe as well as the negative ones, and try to label the more subtle ones in between. The responses in the previous examples illustrate what to say and do when you want to know how your child feels. Not every statement your child makes needs an empathetic response; it's up to you to decide when you want to encourage your child to tell you what's on his mind and in his heart.

Avoiding Communication Traps

When we miss hearing our children, it's often because we have some preprogrammed responses that we use without thinking. Adults unknowingly cut off communication by falling into communication traps. Below is a list of the most common ones:

1. Denying the child's feelings—"You're just tired. You'll feel better in the morning."
2. Philosophizing—"Well, you win some and you lose some."
3. Giving advice—"Here's what you should do."
4. Blaming—"You should have tried harder."
5. Defending the other person—"Well no wonder! You hit her!"

6. Pitying the child—"Oh, you poor baby!"
7. Analyzing the child's behavior—"I think you're trying to feel better by blaming her."

Now consider the seven traps above as you imagine the following situation: A twelve-year-old boy has just returned from a weekend camping trip. He seems troubled as he says he needs to talk about something that happened.

John: Our leader was acting really weird. He showed us *Playboy* magazines and he let us drink beer. At first I thought it was kinda cool, but then he tried to get some of the guys to take their clothes off. He told us we could party like this more often if we didn't tell our parents. The guy is really strange!

Here are reactions from several different parents:

Parent #1: That guy's going to jail for this! And to think that he got the community service award last year. . . . Well, it just makes me sick! You poor baby. Just when you think you can trust somebody, something like this happens!

Parent #2: Oh, I've known Jim for twenty years. Sure, he gets a little wild once in a while, but it's all in fun. Just forget about it.

Parent #3: Obviously he is a very disturbed man who needs sexual gratification from young boys.

Parent #4: You shouldn't have been looking at those *Playboys*. That's why things got out of hand! And you should have been more careful! I told you there were lots of crazies out there!

Parent #5: We need to be forgiving of others, son. Your leader made a mistake. Everybody makes mistakes.

Would you agree that each of these parents fell into one or more of the communication traps I listed earlier? Let's look at how each parent reacted.

Parent #1 immediately gets caught up in his own feelings

rather than helping the boy with his. The parent's sense of shock and horror is understandable, but nothing is being said that will actually help the boy deal with his traumatic experience. Instead of reassuring the boy, this parent has added to the boy's worry about what happened. Also, the parent didn't show compassion or empathy for the son; instead, the parent expressed pity and disgust. The boy may feel confused about turning in his group leader, and the parent's vow to send the leader to jail can only increase the boy's sense of responsibility for betraying the group's secret. Put all of these elements together, and it is easy to see why the son may not want to share his secrets with this parent again.

Parent #2 quickly sets up defenses in order to avoid hearing anything negative. The parent tries to rationalize the group leader's behavior in an effort to make the whole unpleasant conversation end as quickly as possible. By diminishing the boy's upset and by confusing the boy further about what he did or didn't experience, this parent has failed to respond in an open and compassionate way. It is highly unlikely that the child will come to this parent with his troubles the next time.

Parent #3 intellectualizes the incident and dodges both his and his son's emotions by analyzing the situation. This response is likely to be interpreted by the child as cold and uncaring. Rather than feeling supported by the parent, the boy will probably feel emotionally abandoned. He will learn to not seek out his parent when he feels upset because doing so makes him feel *more* alone than he feels already.

Parent #4 assumes a blaming attitude that makes matters worse. Now, in addition to feeling upset, the boy is made to feel guilty and ashamed for his participation. Blaming the victim is a typical psychological defense: it serves to provide us with safe, pat answers when there are none. No child who gets blamed for an upsetting experience such as this would ask his parent to help him again.

Parent #5 philosophizes and offers cliché wisdom instead of empathy and support. Imagine how angry this boy feels when he is told that he must set aside his own feelings and immediately feel compassion and forgiveness toward the youth leader who has betrayed his trust. He gets the message that the leader's behavior was a simple mistake, one that anyone could have made. The parent fails to validate the boy's reality or the seriousness of the incident and instead mouths platitudes that are likely to infuriate the boy. Now the boy has a terrible dilemma; he can either forgive and forget or feel that he is an uncaring, unforgiving human being. The parent leaves no other options open and closes the door on further communication.

In contrast, here is a possible response that avoids all the communication traps and keeps the doors of communication wide open:

Parent: I can hardly believe what you're telling us! No wonder you're upset. Is there anything else you need to tell us?

This parent manages his feelings well from the start. He quickly acknowledges his anger and disbelief and then turns his focus to the son's distress. The parent in no way doubts or questions what the boy has reported or how he is feeling about the incident. He remains calm, does not express his own horror, and shows empathy and understanding for the distress the boy is in. Then, in a matter-of-fact tone, the parent asks for more information. The parent will undoubtedly get it using this open and compassionate response.

If your child comes to you with something she's been told to keep a secret, your ability to listen and manage your feelings can determine whether she feels heard and protected or blamed and guilty. If you imply that what she has done is shameful or bad, her willingness to go to you or any other adult when she's in trouble is decreased, and she is much more likely to keep secrets from you in the future.

However, if you and your child can establish an open, honest, ongoing dialogue, you will be able to create a cushion of emotional safety that will make it easier for her to come to you anytime with *anything*. Be sure you're prepared to hear and believe your child.

To Love and to Cherish

Have you ever caught yourself saying something to your child you swore you'd never say? Or done something you vowed never to do? I used to be an expert on how to avoid these mistakes. Then I became a parent! The truth is, we all make mistakes with our kids, sometimes the same ones our parents made with us. When we're feeling guilty about a thoughtless or uncaring remark, it's important to remember that a single badly handled incident won't ruin your child's self-esteem. At the same time, we need to recognize that angry, critical words day after day can cause children to feel unloved or unworthy.

Think about each of your children as you consider the following questions:

1. What do I appreciate about my child?
2. How do I praise my child for something he/she does well?
3. Do I notice when my child makes an effort or do I mostly notice his/her successes? What do I usually say or do to encourage him/her?
4. In what ways do I communicate to my child that he/she is lovable? What words and phrases do I use?

Were these questions easy or difficult for you to answer? Did you have to think hard to recall what you say or do that conveys your love and approval?

Child specialist Dorothy Corkille Briggs suggests that children need to be cherished, not merely accepted, for who they are. Feeling cherished means knowing that you are valued and precious and special just because you exist. Most of us do cherish our children. But so often that cherishing gets lost and our children fail to feel it. How does this happen? It happens in the day-to-day routines that rob us of seeing the wonder in the world and the people around us. It happens when we are unhappy in our own lives and can't promote happiness in our children. It happens when we inadvertently treat our children as second-class citizens instead of with respect.

Many of our parents were not raised to see children as people. That a child was a person with feelings was a revolutionary concept! A generation later, this concept is the accepted view. But not all parents find it easy to treat their children with respect. If you're wondering whether you're a respectful parent, here's a quick test: Think about how you treat your adult friends. Then ask yourself, "If I treated my friends the same way I treat my children, how many friends would I have left?" Many adults unthinkingly assume that treatment unacceptable for an adult is all right for a child.

For some adults who have never enjoyed the respect of their own parents, it's hard to know exactly what respectful treatment looks and sounds like. Perhaps it's easier to start with what respectful treatment is *not*. It's not making a child feel small, shamed, guilty, nonexistent, or embarrassed. It's not talking down to him, calling him names, or ridiculing him.

How can we be respectful? We are respectful when we see our children as whole human beings with thoughts and feelings as important as our own, by recognizing that children *can* and *do* learn from their mistakes, just as adults do, and by offering acceptance and help rather than criticism when they are confused or troubled.

What we reflect back to our children about themselves truly shapes their identities. We mirror who they are in our eyes, our words, and our behavior toward them. If we distort that mirror with our own problems—with issues we must resolve that have *nothing* to do with them—their inner mirrors will become cracked or clouded. But if our words and deeds reflect "You are worthy of respect," then they will learn to respect themselves and others.

Taking a Self-Inventory

When I conduct my programs around the United States, I ask teachers, nurses, counselors, and other helping professionals to identify their unique gifts. I ask them to tell me what's special about them. You might think that people in these professions would quickly come up with qualities like "ability to listen," "caring about people," or "patience." But that's not what happens. Instead, when I ask this question, only a few can make a list of their strengths. Some people name one or two. Some people struggle to name one special quality. And others draw a complete blank.

I believe that many of us have lost track of our gifts and special qualities along the way to becoming responsible adults. As parents, we feed and clothe our children and do a hundred mundane and often boring tasks to keep our households running smoothly. At the end of each day, we rarely have the time, energy, or inclination to appreciate in what ways we are special or unique. So please take a moment to do that now. You have certain strengths and abilities that are unique to you. Make a list of them. If you have trouble, ask your partner or a friend for their ideas.

What Makes Me Unique

1. _____

2. _____

3. _____

4. _____

5. _____

6. _____

7. _____
   _____
8. _____
   _____
9. _____
   _____
10. _____
   _____

In coming up with your list, you might have heard a voice in your head reminding you what you *don't* have, what you're *not*. This inner voice speaks to you when you—and perhaps other important people in your life or your past—focus on your shortcomings instead of your strengths. You must manage that voice so that you don't inadvertently focus on what's missing in you and then, in turn, focus on what's missing in your children. Just as you have value simply because you are alive, so do your children. Just as you must prize your own uniqueness, you must show your children how to prize theirs.

If it is difficult or impossible to think about yourself in positive terms or if you have trouble seeing the wonderful qualities in your children, you may need to seek some help. Feelings of inadequacy and old emotional issues can—and do—prevent people from being good parents and from enjoying their lives. Counseling can help heal emotional wounds and give you a healthier perspective about yourself and the people you love.

To concentrate on your children's positive qualities, you may need to quiet that negative voice within you. Consciously notice the positive parts of your child's personality separate from her behavior and performance. Too often, performance denies self-worth. Did you ever bring home a report card that wasn't good enough, no matter how many A's were on it? Or played a recital piece that was flawed by an error "you shouldn't have made"? How about the time you owned up to a lie, only to be told that you were a "disappointment" to your parents?

If you have ever felt unloved because you didn't please your parents or because you didn't meet their standards, you know how devastating this can feel. As Dorothy Briggs notes: "Successful performance builds the sense of worthwhileness; being cherished as a person nurtures the feeling of being loved."

Maybe you agree with what I'm saying, but you're wondering how it's possible to always look for the best and maintain a positive outlook. Frankly, it's not possible. But each day, if you can catch yourself and can quickly notice when you're being judgmental or unforgiving, or selling your kids short, then you can simply stop and start over. As I mentioned earlier, our children are willing to forgive us when we do something wrong. We just need to know what we are trying to do right and be willing to do it. If this seems to be an impossible challenge, consider professional counseling or a parenting class to bolster your own self-esteem and coping skills.

Let your child know each day that you love her—that you think of her and appreciate her for who she is. Leave messages on the mirror. Put a little surprise under his pillow. Give him a hug and tell him why he's so special to you. Whatever you do, show your love and affection. Think of creative and special ways to let your children know how important they are to you. Don't worry about spoiling your children with too many hugs or by telling them you love them too often. Remember, your child is more at risk if she doesn't feel loved or appreciated.

Take time to enjoy your children. On Mother's Day, my daughter reminded me that it's the little things we do together that matter the most. Share treasured memories together, sing in the car, laugh together, shed your role as an adult and learn how to play! Risk being human and foolish and silly with your children. These intimate moments leave your child with emotional reserves when you are apart. As a wise colleague of mine says, "Give your children the next best thing to your being there. Give them themselves."

Encouragement and Praise

"Catch 'em at being good," the saying goes. Do you notice and praise your children's positive efforts? It's easy to notice their big accomplishments, but it takes conscious effort to remember to praise the small steps along the way. For example, let's say your child is learning her phone number, which is important safety information she needs to memorize, and she recites part of it correctly. Which style of responding is most like yours?

Dad #1: Great.
Dad #2: You only got half of it right.
Dad #3: You've really got that first part down. Would you like some help with the last part?

Vague, general praise like "great," "beautiful," or "fantastic" really doesn't mean much to a child. Often such praise is given with little or no thought, and the child doesn't receive the message behind it at all. Dad #1's halfhearted comment is not likely to convey his pleasure or the pride he feels in watching his daughter do a good job. Dad #2's response focuses on the negative and is likely to discourage the child from trying harder. In the third example, the father offers specific comments based on the child's observable behavior. Dad #3's encouragement gives the child a realistic sense of her abilities and strengths and supports her to finish the important job that she has started.

It's also a good idea to express your pleasure about the effort she's making.

Dad: I'm happy to hear you've been practicing your phone number. Learning your phone number is an important responsibility and you're handling it very well.

With this kind of specific encouragement, the child gets the message that she's a responsible person and that practicing is important. When we show our appreciation for our children's efforts and encourage specific behaviors, our children are more willing to repeat the desired behavior. If we praise them in this way, they learn how to praise themselves and gain insight into who they are.

Here is some practice in offering specific praise and encouragement. Let's say Jeff calls you when his ride home falls through. You have told him to do this if he ever misses a ride or the bus leaves without him.

Jeff: Mom, can you come pick us up?
Mom: I thought Jason's mother was going to pick you up.
Jeff: Yeah, but something must have happened. She's a half hour late.

OK, now it's your turn. You are right in the middle of something and annoyed that Jason's mother didn't hold up her end of the agreement. Try filling in the blanks with your own words, keeping in mind that you want to encourage and praise Jeff for his responsible behavior.

Mom: I'm annoyed that Jason's mother didn't come but I'm glad

_____

_____

_____

When I know I can count on you to _____

_____

_____, I feel confi-
dent about letting you go places with friends. You acted
very _____.

Here are a couple of possible responses to Jeff:

Mom: I'm annoyed that Jason's mother didn't come, but I'm
glad you remembered to call me and didn't walk home.
When I know I can count on you to use your good judg-

ment, I feel confident about letting you go places with your friends. You acted very responsibly.

or

Mom: I'm glad you called me and didn't walk home. You used good judgment. I'll be there in ten minutes.

The parent consciously manages her own irritation and praises Jeff for the specific behavior that she wants to encourage. Jeff ends up feeling that he is responsible and trustworthy. Also, he gets the message that he has earned future privileges based on his responsible behavior. Granting children privileges based on their demonstrated behavior—and making one contingent upon the other—sets kids up for success and avoids placing them in situations they can't handle.

In this chapter, I've suggested how to create family environments where children can discuss anything and assertiveness is valued and encouraged. We've talked about what you can do to ensure that your children feel loved and cherished and how those feelings are distinct from feeling capable and competent. By establishing open communication and by offering specific praise, we're raising children to feel good about themselves. We're raising self-respecting kids who are less likely to become victims.

Key Points

When Listening to Children . . .

- Eliminate distractions.
- Listen quietly and attentively.
- Use words and facial expressions that encourage them to continue sharing their thoughts and feelings.

When Talking to Children . . .

- Maintain good eye contact.
- Use short, simple sentences.

- Speak more slowly than usual.
- Use vocabulary they can understand.

When Responding to Children's Feelings . . .

- Tune in to how your *child* is experiencing the situation, and put your own feelings on hold while you're listening.
- Give your child's feeling a name to help him understand what he is experiencing; for example, "Seems like you're feeling confused about this."
- Believe and accept the child's feelings to promote trust and open communication.

When Promoting Children's Self-Esteem . . .

- Tell and show your children that you love and appreciate them.
- Catch them doing something well and praise them for it.
- Show them that they are worthy of respect.

When Praising and Encouraging Children . . .

- Praise their efforts as well as their accomplishments.
- Praise specific behaviors and avoid general, nonspecific praise.
- Use praise to encourage responsible behavior.
- Offer realistic praise to help children identify their strengths and abilities.

CHAPTER 4

Why Scare Tactics Don't Work

Recently a mother of two young children said to me, "I hate having to teach my children to be afraid." If, like her, you feel resigned to using scare tactics to teach personal safety, you may have a little trouble believing what I'm about to say, but here it is: *Scare tactics don't work.*

The belief that we must scare kids in order to protect them from harm is a myth, a misconception. What *is* true is that we need to teach them *exactly what to do* in order to stay safe in a variety of situations. This means shifting from alarming warnings to teaching specific information and skills. For many adults, shifting from what *not* to do to what to do represents a big change in how they talk to kids.

Do you remember hearing, "Don't cross a busy street. You'll get hit by a car!"? Or, were you taught, "Cross only when the light is green" or "Look both ways before you cross the street"? The "don't" statement above told you what *not* to do and threatened that you would get hit by a car if you ignored the warning about crossing busy streets. In essence, it taught you to be *afraid* of traffic. The "do" statement taught you how to cross the street safely. It contained no threats or alarming consequences and gave you clear, specific directions to follow.

Changing the way you talk—shifting from "don'ts" to

"dos"—takes some conscious thought and effort. Maybe you think something so subtle can't make a lot of difference. But it does. What you say and *how* you say it has a direct impact on whether your child stays safe or whether she becomes a victim.

The Negative Impact of Fear

Do you unwittingly teach your children what to be afraid of instead of what to do to stay safe? One afternoon, I observed my daughter's teacher telling his students to wait for their parents inside the building rather than on the steps that led down to a busy street. When one of the students asked why, the teacher said, "Because someone could snatch you right off the steps!" His intentions were to protect the children, but his words unnecessarily alarmed them.

As I watched my daughter's friends scurry back into the building, many of them glancing nervously over their shoulders, I thought about how often we resort to scaring children into obeying our rules. Yes, it was appropriate for this teacher to tell the kids that they couldn't wait outside for their parents. But he could have gotten the children inside by offering a nonalarming explanation like "It's hard for me to keep an eye on everyone when you're outside" or "It's best to wait inside rather than on a busy street."

I must say I've heard parents use these kinds of explanations too, usually when they're feeling a loss of control in a situation. Scare tactics are used as a last resort to get children to comply. The mother who can't get her son to come down out of a tree, for example, gets frustrated and says, "OK, but don't blame me if you fall and break your leg!" The father who can't get his daughter to wear her bicycle helmet gets angry and shouts, "When you crack your head open on the sidewalk and have to have stitches, don't come crying to me!" Perhaps if we felt more secure in gaining our children's cooperation, we wouldn't resort to emotional warfare to regain control over them. Manipulating children into obeying our rules by instilling fear in them is not only unfair; it can have serious consequences.

Remember those students waiting to get picked up? It's easy to imagine that the next time they are waiting for their parents, most of them will feel at least some apprehensiveness about standing anywhere near those steps. Now some of you may be thinking, "Good! That will remind them to get inside!" But it doesn't work that way. When we scare kids with graphic details of what will happen if they don't heed our warnings, they are unlikely to remember any useful information and are more likely to remember to feel *afraid*.

Fear is disabling. Kids can become paralyzed by fear. You undermine their ability to respond safely in dangerous situations when you give them fear-contaminated facts; instead of approaching dangerous situations with street-smart awareness and self-protective skills, they develop an automatic fear trigger that goes off in the face of danger. The result is that they can't respond quickly and safely because they're terrified. They can't use critical information or think on their feet in a dangerous situation because they're frozen with fear.

It's All in Their Minds

Sometimes, as I pass children playing on the sidewalk, I see them look at me with eyes as big as saucers. I can almost read their minds, a blur of parental warnings spinning in their heads as I get closer: "Don't talk to strangers." "You can't trust anyone!" "Kidnappers are everywhere!" These fearful—and inaccurate—warnings are not what our children need to be thinking about when they are allowed to play in their front yards. What they need to have in mind are protective strategies to use if a stranger acts inappropriately. What exactly does "inappropriately" mean?

Acting in a menacing or odd way is one definition. But it doesn't accurately describe how many abductors act. We must remember that many abductors and molesters appear friendly, interested, and completely *nonthreatening*. They are expert in *not* acting like strangers so that children will lower their guard. For example, a man convinces a child that he is a friend of the family and has come to give the child a ride to the hospital because his mother has been in an accident. He acts concerned and reassuring and expresses his desire to help. Another stranger, pretending to be lost, coaxes a child over to his car to help him find a street on the map. He looks confused, but by no means dangerous.

Criminals know how to take advantage of children's kindness and naïveté. So, to counter their ploys, we must teach kids how to respond to strangers who act overly interested or appeal for help. Our message to children about strangers must be that anything beyond a brief greeting should be treated with extreme caution.

Also, remember that "Don't talk to strangers" is not really what you mean. You *want* your children to be able to ask for help if they need it. If they develop a fear of strangers, they will be isolated in an emergency. Kids need to turn to adults—even ones they don't know—if they are in trouble. In chapter 8, I'll show you how to teach children to go to "helping people" or "safe strangers" when they are in trouble.

While our fears may be the result of the deep love and concern we feel for our children, it is our responsibility to manage them. We need to be calm and matter-of-fact when we talk about personal safety with our kids. Talk about personal safety in the same way you talk about other safety rules. State personal-safety rules the same way you would say, "Keep your finger out of electrical sockets." You don't need to tell your son he could die if he put his finger in the socket in order to keep him safe. You simply need to give him straightforward rules to follow without going into detail about the consequences. Remember, when children respond safely in a dangerous situation it's because they can recall clear information, *not* their parents' fears.

I read about a twelve-year-old girl in Pennsylvania who outsmarted a would-be abductor by keeping her wits about her. She was walking to school when a man started walking alongside her. "Do you see my gun?" he asked. She nodded. "Do every-thing I say and you'll be OK," he said. The man told her to walk down the street with him; then he turned down another street and pointed to his truck. "I want you to get into that pickup," he told her. She realized that getting into that truck meant she would be in even greater danger. All the while she continued to nod compliantly, she was calculating her plan of escape. As they walked toward his truck, she started to fake an asthma attack, wheezing and struggling for breath. She asked him if she could sit down for a moment on a bench. As she started to take off her backpack, he tried to grab her, but she pulled away; he got her backpack instead. Then she ran as fast as she could for help. Later that day, Lewis S. Lent Jr. was arrested and was linked to a string of child kidnappings and slayings in the area.

Why was this girl successful in getting away? Because she knew how to manage her fear. She knew how to stay calm and rational and used critical thinking to plan her escape. Kids can be taught how to become critical thinkers when in danger. But if we don't manage our own fears, or if we scare them with horror stories, they won't be able to use their street smarts when it really counts. In fact, they are likely to clutch or freeze in fear.

Reacting vs. Teaching

Have you noticed that whenever a horrible tragedy is paraded before us on television or in the newspapers, we suddenly increase our surveillance of our children? We intensify our reminders and warnings. Some parents, having never men-tioned personal safety before, hurriedly instruct their children about the consequences of various behaviors. The obvious fear and concern they feel are quickly transmitted to the children. And fear inhibits both critical thinking and learning.

Imagine what it's like from the child's perspective. Your child sees how scared you are and thinks, "Gee, if this scares Dad, it *must* be bad!" At a time when your children desperately need to pay attention to your instructions, you may be so negative and emotional that you inhibit their ability to listen to you. When children pick up on your fears, they conjure up vivid, frightening images. And young children, especially, believe that things that they hear about really do happen—and *will happen*—to them! So instead of hearing and remembering the information you're trying to teach, they're having explicit fantasies about terrible people doing terrible things to them. Later, if they need to recall and use critical safety strategies, their imaginations are likely to go into overdrive again and they won't be able to respond safely. Our runaway emotions *can and do* get in the way of safeguarding our children.

Presenting personal-safety information in response to our heightened state of anxiety is the least effective method to use in teaching children. Ideally, the discussion of safety issues needs to be interwoven with other information that we wish to teach our children. We'll talk about how to do this in chapters 5 and 6.

A Reassuring View

As our children grow, it's challenging to reassure them that the world is filled with people who are dedicated to their protection and well-being. Sometimes, in our concern, we forget that the majority of people are trustworthy and caring when it comes to kids. Conveying a healthy sense of trust is dependent on your own attitudes and beliefs. For example, if you are someone who has difficulty trusting others, your words and actions may teach your child to believe that the world consists of largely dangerous or unscrupulous people. On the other hand, if you believe everyone is kind and caring, you're ignoring the realities of modern life. You can't let your children assume that all people have their best interests at heart. It's simply not true.

How do we convey a healthy sense of trust to our children and a balanced view of our world? Well, for one thing, as they grow, we must continue to reinforce the notion that *most* people are trustworthy. When they're old enough to understand that there are exceptions to this rule, we tell them that *some* people act inappropriately with children and a *few* people cause children serious harm. Then we teach them what to do if they should ever encounter such persons, all the while reassuring them that *most* people do not behave in such hurtful ways.

We must talk about the likelihood of our kids coming to any harm in terms they can understand. For example, we can use analogies: "You know how once in a while there's a hurricane or an earthquake or a tornado? They're pretty unusual but they do happen. Well, that's about how often a child might get kidnapped. Most of the time, though, kids are safe."

It is unnecessary and potentially damaging to tell children about the dangers in their world before they can understand them. Consider how young children need to believe in certain "truths" like the Easter Bunny and Santa Claus. They also believe that Mommy and Daddy know everything and have magical powers to "make it all better." Children believe in absolutes in the beginning: good and bad, right and wrong. It does no good to paint a picture of the world that they are simply unwilling or unable to see.

For example, I tell my seven-year-old daughter that if she is ever in trouble, she can count on a "helping person" like a policeman to help her. Do I also tell her about the policeman who was recently convicted of child molestation? No! But as she becomes a little more independent, I'll teach her that some people masquerade as law enforcement officers to trick children. At that point I'll teach her how to distinguish between someone in uniform who is trying to help and someone who may be trying to coax her into his car. Right now, however, I want her to feel secure knowing that there are people who can help her if she is lost or afraid.

Do I scare my thirteen-year-old nephew, who rides the city trains and buses, about pedophiles who hang out at bus and train stations looking for adolescent boys? Of course not. Since he's been taught how to respond to inappropriate overtures from strangers, a reminder to stay alert and aware is sufficient.

Is it possible to know in advance what scares kids? Yes, I

think so. But even a well-intentioned organization can make a mistake. In 1984, the National Center for Missing and Exploited Children launched a campaign to put photos of missing children on milk cartons. Soon they learned that these photos were upsetting children around the country. Each morning at breakfast, thousands of children stared at photos of kids who had been taken from their parents. Each morning thousands of kids got scared. So, the Center pulled the photos from the milk cartons. Now these photos appear on the back of advertisements that are mailed to *adults*.

As children grow and are gradually exposed to a broader cross section of people, they must be prepared for what and who they may encounter. However, every time we share difficult truths with them, keep in mind that our goal is to *reinforce* their sense of security, not to destroy it. With each step they take toward independence, we need to give them a new piece of information about their world and about the people in it. But we must do it thoughtfully and carefully, unfolding one layer of reality after another over time. And, as we teach, we must consciously convey our enduring faith in people, at least in the *majority* of them. This approach helps children develop a realistic sense of security and a balanced attitude about the dangers in their world.

Managing the Media at Home

How often have you picked up a newspaper and read about a child being kidnapped or murdered and thought, "How horrible! That guy's sick! He needs to be put away for good!"? Do you sometimes make a comment like this within earshot of your children? Many parents do. Whether your children learn about child-related crimes from you or whether they get their information from television, radio, or the newspaper, the risk of overexposing our children to reports of crime and violence is high.

We can't allow children unlimited access to the news for two basic reasons. First, the media make no effort to avoid words and pictures that alarm children. In fact, crime is usually reported in sensational and graphic terms. Newspaper-selling headlines like POLICE OFFICER ARRESTED ON CHILD MOLESTATION CHARGES land on the front page, where our children can easily read them. Second, your child may be emotionally traumatized by horrific news stories.

In a 1994 study done by the Psycho-Social Treatment Laboratory at Stanford University's School of Medicine, television news was linked to stress in one thousand schoolchildren in California, Oregon, and Utah. While numerous studies in recent years have demonstrated that children often suffer harmful long-term effects from watching the fictional violence they see on television, this continuing study focuses on what happens to kids who see real-life events on television. The Stanford researchers are finding that real-life violence reported on TV news may have just as powerful an effect on young emotions as grisly fictional crime shows or actually experiencing a terrifying incident. Preliminary findings strongly suggest that parents should prevent young children—and those who tend to be fearful or anxious—from watching the six o'clock news. Also, parents shouldn't leave the newspaper on the kitchen table, where small children are likely to see it.

Real-life crimes on television don't seem very far away to children who are continually bombarded with "news updates" and "special reports." Because TV news coverage is not aimed at

---

If your child is overexposed to reports of crime and violence, she may exhibit one or more of the following stress-related reactions:

- Nightmares or bad dreams
- Fearfulness
- Anxiety
- Inability to concentrate

children, we must be vigilant about protecting our children from hearing and seeing too much of it. This also goes for television shows like *America's Most Wanted* that offer highly detailed and sensationalized accounts of crimes.

At what age can kids handle this kind of exposure? A twelve-year-old may be as likely to have a nightmare after watching a gory news report as a six-year-old. The answer has less to do with age than it does with your child's ability to hold on to the fact that the world is both good and bad—at the same time. Developing this perspective takes time and emotional, as well as intellectual, maturity.

Another way we can shield our children from overexposure is to keep our own emotions in check. Here's an example of how one mother deals with her reaction to a story in the newspaper. She turns to her ten-year-old son and says: "I just read about a girl being kidnapped in front of a store because a man took her bicycle and persuaded her to come over and get it. She was with a friend, too. These maniacs are getting bolder and crazier all the time! It's just not safe for you to ride your bike around here, even with a friend."

How do you think the boy is likely to feel after hearing his mother's emotion-laden reaction to this incident? Is she teaching him any valuable information or is she projecting her fears onto her son? When we don't manage our fears and consider the impact of our words on our kids, we often end up sounding just like this parent. The mother has every reason to feel concerned, but she needs to discuss her feelings with another *adult*, not her son.

When a brutal reminder of dangerous situations is flashed before us on television, we may become more anxious about our children's safety. But look at how the mother talks about this news story when she is mindful of the fact that she doesn't want *her* worries to become her *son's*:

Mother: Eric, what would you do if you parked your bike and when you came back to get it, a stranger had it?

Eric: Well, I'd tell him to give it back to me.

Mother: But what if this stranger told you he was thinking of getting a bike like yours for his son and just wanted to look at it. Then he asks you to come over and explain something to him.

Eric: Well, since he's just looking at my bike because he wants to buy one, I'd probably go over and talk with him.

Mother: OK, let's talk about that for a minute. What did we say was a safe way to act with strangers?

Eric: Don't get too close to them.

Mother: Right. And remember I told you that it's OK for strangers to smile and say "Hi," but then they should move on. Here's a stranger that's taken something of yours and is asking you a lot of questions. He's not acting the way strangers are supposed to act. It wouldn't be a good idea to answer or go over to him.

Eric: But he's got my bike!

Mother: Exactly. If a stranger takes something of yours, your safest reaction would be "Hey, something's wrong here!" and then to get away and go for help.

Eric: Like tell him, "Hey! Put my bike down right now!" and if he doesn't, run and tell somebody?

Mother: Exactly. Now you're thinking. That's a much safer solution. Can I count on you to remember that when I let you ride your bike to the store?

Eric: Sure, Mom.

In this example, the mother turns her emotional reactions into a positive means of protecting her son. She recognizes her fears and uses them as reminders to teach personal-safety information. She feels apprehensive about allowing him to ride his bike around the neighborhood and wants some assurance that he won't get coaxed away by a stranger who feigns interest in his bike.

Notice that the mother doesn't project her feelings into the conversation. She may be upset by the news story, but rather than allowing her feelings to dictate her behavior, she takes a moment to gather her thoughts. Then, she opens with a "What if . . . ?" question and poses a hypothetical situation rather than talking about the kidnapping directly. (If, however, the *boy* brought up the incident, the mother would be obligated to deal with her son's questions about the kidnapping.) Notice that when Eric tells his mother he would help the stranger, she immediately realizes that Eric would be vulnerable in this situation. Instead of reacting with frustration or fear, she simply reviews how he is supposed to interact with strangers.

By the end of the conversation the boy is better prepared and the mother feels reassured knowing that Eric will be able to respond safely if he should ever encounter this situation. *And not once was it necessary for this parent to share any of the details of the crime reported in the newspaper with her son.*

The mother wisely uses the news story as an opportunity to reinforce specific safety skills for her son and to gain some peace of mind for herself. This example illustrates how we can use the news to teach our children valuable safety skills. The mother creates a "teachable moment" to review important safety information with her son. By thinking about what it is she wants her son to learn before she brings up the incident, she turns an anxiety-provoking situation into a productive one.

The Nickelodeon TV channel recently aired a special news program featuring Linda Ellerbee. (This cable channel is geared to grade-school-age children and offers a wide variety of programming, from educational programs to game shows.) When I first saw the title, "Stranger Danger," I was skeptical. As I mentioned earlier, clever titles used to promote personal-safety programs often perpetuate myths and misinformation; at their worst, they feed on kids' fears. *Stranger* and *danger* shouldn't be linked together in children's minds.

Despite my reservations, I made a date to watch the program with my seven-year-old daughter. Before the show started, I made a mental note that we would turn it off if I felt any of the information was too scary or graphic for her. After the first few minutes, however, I was relieved to hear the reassuring and moderate tone of the program. Not once were alarming words used, and when videotaped case examples were shown, the young viewers were reminded that all the people involved were actors. I also watched to see if my daughter popped her thumb in her mouth, a sure signal to me that she was feeling uneasy.

After the show, we discussed what she had seen and heard. It was a great way to check out what she understood and to clarify any information that was unclear, and I had a perfect opportunity to practice using nonalarming words and phrases. I was pleased with how much she had learned and seemed to understand. The next day, she brought up the program again and asked me another question. And then, when she saw there was going to be an encore presentation of the special, she said she wanted to watch it again!

Be willing and available to introduce your children to television and reading material that appropriately educates kids about personal safety. Be sure the material steers clear of scare tactics and be ready to clear up any misinformation that might be presented. Also, use the TV program or book to begin a question-and-answer session. Remember, for real learning to take place, you need to discuss how the ideas in the book or the TV program are relevant to your child.

The Power of Your Words

In this section you will gain practice in distinguishing between words and phrases that *scare* children about the dangers of the world and words and phrases that *teach* children personal-safety information. Consider the following example:

Father: I've been looking everywhere for you! You know you're not supposed to leave the yard without permission! You could have been kidnapped or killed! Haven't I told you there are lots of crazies out there, just looking for kids like you?!

Here are nine tips for how to deal with news reports of violence and crime:

1. Share your reactions with another *adult*, not with your child.
2. Don't discuss a particular crime unless your child asks about it.
3. If your child initiates a discussion, share as few details about the crime as possible and mostly listen.
4. Use the incident to teach or reinforce safety concepts.
5. Have young children play in another room while you are watching the news or watch the late news after they are asleep.
6. Protect young children from scary photos and alarming headlines by storing the newspaper out of their reach.
7. Do not watch reality-based crime programs or "docudramas" like *America's Most Wanted* with your children.
8. If your children are upset by something they have read or seen, offer reassurance.
9. Watch television programs with your kids that are designed to educate them about their personal safety. Discuss them afterward.

It's easy to understand how this parent became so frightened. I'm sure we've all had the experience of turning around and suddenly realizing our child is not there. It's happened to me. Your heart begins to pound, and you run in every direction, looking and calling for your child. It can be a terrifying experience. Then, when you do find her, you're filled with a huge sense of relief—and some frustration and anger. You can't wait to get your hands on her. But why? For what? I ask parents, "What is it you're going to do when you get your hands on your child?" And some of them say, "I'm going to shake some sense into her!" or "I'm going to show him how worried and upset he made me!"

As I discussed earlier, it doesn't work to try to scare your children into being more careful or to make them feel guilty if they're not. But it's totally understandable that when your child disappears, you get scared. The father in this example used alarming words and threatened the child with horrible consequences for breaking the rule about leaving the yard. After frantically searching for his son, he was very upset and he wanted him to know it. But did he have to frighten his son to communicate this?

The father needs to take a deep breath, put his feelings aside for a moment, and focus on what it is he wants his son to do differently next time. Notice how much more effective he is now:

Father: I was scared and worried when I couldn't find you. The safety rule is that you need to ask permission to leave the yard. You broke the rule, so you'll need to come inside for the rest of the afternoon. Tomorrow, if you are willing to follow our safety rule, you can play outside again.

This time he sounds more in charge of himself and the situation. He's in a much better position to review the family safety rules and reinforce the kind of behavior he expects from his child. There is a major difference between the first and second responses. In the first example, the father confuses *scaring* his child with *teaching* his child. In the second example, he consciously does the following things:

- Manages his feelings
- Focuses on what his son needs to learn
- Uses nonalarming words
- Speaks in a matter-of-fact way
- Reinforces the safety rule or information

Managing your feelings and staying aware of what you're trying to teach will help you get safety information across to your children. To be effective, you'll also need to use words that teach children how to be safe rather than words that alarm or scare them.

In the next example, decide whether the grandmother is teaching or scaring her grandchild.

Grandmother: Even normal-looking people can be child molesters and sex perverts! If anyone tries to touch you and you don't like it, tell them to stop and come tell me about it! Child molesters can be anybody—friends, relatives, teachers, even police officers! Don't trust anyone who tries to get too friendly with you!

Well, what do you think? This grandparent has good intentions and is trying to teach important safety skills, but listen to some of the words she's using: *child molesters, sex perverts*. She's contaminating what she's teaching with alarming words and by being too dramatic. Notice the difference when she tries to be more aware of how she's communicating.

Grandmother: This is hard for me to talk about because I get so angry that there are people in the world who do bad things to kids. But it's important for you to know that there are adults who might try to trick you with lots of attention or presents and then ask you to undress, or to touch their "privates" or let them touch yours. It's against the law for an adult to treat a child that way. If any adult touches you in a way that feels confusing or wrong, even if they have told you to keep it a secret, get out of there, and tell me right away.

This time the grandmother stays away from alarming words and phrases. She focuses on what she's trying to teach and keeps her own emotions under control. She matter-of-factly describes what behavior to look for and tells the girl exactly what she can do to protect herself. Also, notice that the grandmother uses the word *privates* because that's the commonly used language in the family and she knows her grand-daughter understands what it means. The grandmother offers some essential information that all children need to know: molesting children is against the law. Because of her grand-mother's open and calm manner, the child would feel safe enough to ask more questions or to come to her in the event of a troubling incident.

To teach personal safety effectively, you need to be conscious of what's the best possible way to explain something to your children, given their age and level of understanding. For exam-ple, the grandmother didn't use the word *molest*. She said, "touches you in a way that feels confusing or wrong." She also avoided the emotionally charged term *sex pervert* and instead said, "ask[s] you to undress, or to touch their 'privates' or let them touch yours." It's not that you can't use words such as *molest* and *pervert* with older children. You just need to define and describe these terms clearly in the beginning; otherwise, children are likely to become confused or miss important infor-mation about how they should behave to protect themselves. In general, describing behavior for children is preferable to using words that tend to carry an emotional charge, even if it takes a little longer to explain with a sentence or a phrase.

Words That Create Fear or Confusion	Words That Teach or Reassure
Don't talk to strangers.	Here's how strangers should behave.
There are crazy people out there!	Most people are trustworthy.
Someone might kidnap you.	You will be safe if . . .
Parks are too dangerous for kids!	If anyone approaches you . . .
You can't trust anyone these days!	You can ask for help from . . .

I Have a Question . . .

If you are promoting open and safe communication, your child will come to you with questions. The following examples are some common words that you will need to define for your children. They are followed by one possible descriptive phrase that would neither scare nor alarm most children. Some of the descriptive phrases assume that your children already have some general information about sex.

When you use any of the descriptive phrases listed below, your child may ask, "What does that mean?" so you need to be ready with another nonalarming answer. And, just as in teaching children about sex, it's best to let the child's level of interest and curiosity determine how far the conversation goes. You don't want to overwhelm children with too much information at one time.

Words That Need to Be Defined	Nonalarming Descriptive Phrases
Kidnap	Force you to go with them
Rape	Force you to have intercourse/sex
Molest	When an adult touches or fondles a child's private parts for sexual pleasure
Kiddie-porn	Taking or looking at photos of partially dressed or naked children for sexual pleasure
Sex offenders	People who have been convicted and/or jailed for sex-related crimes

Suppose your seven-year-old asks, "What does molest mean?" Here are some possible ways to respond:

"First tell me what you think it means so I can understand what you already know."

"I think we have a book that would help me explain this to you. Would you like to read it with me?"

"Molesting is when an adult tries to touch your private parts. Have you ever heard about that?"

Any of these answers would be appropriate, depending on how much your child understands, how much you know about the subject, and how comfortable you are discussing it. There is no shame, by the way, in reaching for a book at these difficult moments. I've suggested several good ones that you can share with your children in the Resources section of this book.

And, while you may be expecting a brief question-and-answer session, don't be surprised if you find yourself in a lengthy discussion. Be prepared in case your child has been saving up a lot of questions. The following conversation is adapted from *What Should I Tell the Kids?* by Ava Siegler, Ph.D.:

Jimmy: What's incest?

Dad: Sometimes very disturbed adults try to have sex with girls or boys they know. The worst thing of all is when a parent tries to use a child in this way. That's called incest.

Jimmy: Why doesn't the child just say she won't do it if it's bad?

Dad: Sometimes the child is too afraid to say no to a parent and too upset to talk to anyone about incest because, even though he might know it's wrong, he still loves him, and he's afraid he'll get in trouble.

Jimmy: But he's bad.

Dad: You're right, but sometimes kids are afraid to tell anyone because they feel maybe it's *their* fault their parent is acting this way. But it's *never,* ever the child's fault when a grown-up sexually abuses them.

Jimmy: Why doesn't he tell his mommy?

Dad: You're right! Children *always,* always need to tell a

grown-up they trust—their mommy or their teacher or their grandpa—about what's happening. Then they can get help to stop it.

I think we'd all agree that the hardest sexual abuse of all to talk about is incest. The father in this example managed his discomfort well so that he could be calm and helpful. By focusing on his child's questions and by managing his feelings, he is effective in guiding the conversation so that it serves his son's needs. He informs and explains, he offers compassion and understanding, and he reassures the boy about specific ways he can protect himself from an incestuous relationship with an adult. Could you tell how old the boy was from how the father spoke to him? The boy in this example was eight years old.

Even if you're hoping this subject will never come up, at some point you'll need to prepare an explanation for your children. More than likely, they will need your help in comprehending this incomprehensible experience.

Now take a look at the following statements. Each one contains an alarming word or phrase. Think about what you could say instead that would teach your child what she would need to know but wouldn't scare her.

Instead of *"You can't go to the park by yourself. Someone might kidnap you!"* say, _____

_____

Instead of *"You can't trust anyone. Molesters look just like normal people,"* say, _____

_____

Instead of *"Murderers and rapists look for friendly children, so don't talk to anyone!"* say, _____

_____

Now review your responses. Are there any words that might alarm your child? Did you manage to successfully keep your feelings out of what you were trying to teach? Here are some possible responses:

> Instead of *"You can't go to the park by yourself. Someone might kidnap you!"* say, *"Our safety rule is that you stay with a buddy at all times if you go to the park without an adult. Can I count on you to do that?"*
>
> Instead of *"You can't trust anyone. Molesters look just like normal people,"* say, *"If anyone ever touches you in a way that you don't like or that makes you uncomfortable, even if it's a friend or relative, I want you to tell me right away."*
>
> Instead of *"Murderers and rapists look for friendly children, so don't talk to anyone!"* say, *"Remember to be cautious about strangers. If someone doesn't move on after saying hello or keeps coming closer, run away and get some help."*

How do your answers compare? Did you teach specific, clear information? Did you avoid warnings and threats?

Try saying these responses aloud. Get feedback about the way you look and sound, either by looking in the mirror or having someone listen to you. What's the expression on your face when you speak? Does your voice sound matter-of-fact? Listen to the tone of your voice. If you look or sound alarmed, try coming across in a more neutral way.

Also, if you discovered that it was difficult to manage your discomfort when you thought or spoke about these concepts, make a note of the ones that caused you trouble. Make a list of the words or visual images that make you uncomfortable and discuss them with another adult. Be honest about your fears and worries. You may need to desensitize yourself through repetition and by overrehearsing. If you repeat the word *incest* fifty times, for example, it's unlikely that you will be as bothered by it the last time you say it as you were the first time. Remember, ultimately you're not required to feel calm and matter-of-fact when you discuss personal safety. You just have to *act* that way.

While it's true that these communication skills take practice, there's no better way to develop confidence and comfort in teaching safety information. Communicating so consciously and carefully may feel a little awkward at first. I promise you it will get easier with practice.

Key Points

- Identify your fears and share them with another adult, not with your child.
- During safety conversations, focus on what it is your child needs to learn rather than on your feelings and reactions.
- Develop words and phrases to use that teach caution without creating fear.
- Practice communicating safety concepts until you look and sound calm and confident.
- Ask young children what they already understand so you know where to begin.
- Start with brief, simple answers; then wait for your child to ask for more information before you continue.
- Use your child's words and language whenever possible.
- When introducing new terms, have a simple definition ready that they can easily understand.
- If you develop safe and open communication, your child will come to you with questions and concerns; be prepared for them.

CHAPTER 5

What You Need to Know About Your Kids—and Sex Offenders

I wrote the following poem for the Family 2000 Conference, a national conference on parenting. Titled "Everything You Wanted to Know About Your Child in 2 Minutes or Less," it gives you an *extremely* brief overview of child development.

The warm sweet breath of the infant in your arms
Swaddled close to your breast, dreaming peacefully
Awakens as if for the first time, as it starts to understand
There is more to life than sleeping and eating . . .
Lifting its head, curious, fascinated
Sitting up, reaching, rolling
Creeping, crawling
Banging, bumping
Crashing, falling
Breaking, trashing,
Messing, bawling
Teething, weaning,
Strained bananas on the ceiling

Drooling, dropping
Never stopping
Your toddler!

Catch your breath
For before you stands a preschooler
With an arsenal of personalities, demands, and PASSIONS!
Singing, dancing
Wild romancing
Dressing up and messing up
Building, breaking
Cooking, baking
Running, climbing
Amazing timing
Monsters and bad guys
Rainbow Brite
Scary nightmares
"Leave on the light!"
Oh joy! Oh celebration!
They discover masturbation!

Well, you've made it to grade school
And now it's time for . . .
Homework, hobbies, overnights
Unrelenting sibling fights
Parents Night, cupcakes
Colds and tummy aches
Dentists and doctors
Books left in lockers
Car pools
Trouble at school
Best friends on Monday
Betrayed by Sunday
Tears and moping
Tired of coping

"Stop your swearing!"
"What are you wearing?!"
"Turn that down, the music's blaring!"
Boyfriends, girlfriends
What do I see?
Early signs of puberty?!

Clothes shopping
Mall hopping
Hanging out
3-day pout
AIDS and sexuality
Welcome to reality
So much pressure to achieve
One more year before they leave
"What kind of curfew is 11 PM?!"
"He's not my boyfriend, he's just a friend!"
"I'm not a child!"
"You don't care!"
"Can I have the car?"
"That's not fair!"
"I'm dumb and ugly!"
"I don't drink beer!"
"Mom! Dad! I need you!"
"I'm outta' here!"

In reality, our children don't fast forward through all these ages and stages. But, as parents, there are times when that's what it *feels* like. There will definitely be periods when you and your child will have trouble getting along, when it's hard to communicate. Then, just when you feel like giving up, your child will move on to a new stage and seem to change overnight. There's no doubt about it. At times parenting can feel like a roller-coaster ride.

Understanding what you can expect from children at various

ages and stages can slow down the roller coaster of emotions and level out some of the dips and sharp turns you and your child might otherwise encounter. I can't count the number of times I've calmed myself down by remembering, "This behavior—however obnoxious or annoying—is normal for this age." On countless occasions, I've been able to defuse a situation simply because I knew not to confuse developmentally appropriate behavior with plain naughtiness.

Knowing at what ages children experience great emotional disequilibrium can also help you weather the storms ahead. There are definite stages during which even the most delightful kids, because of developmental turmoil, become unreasonable, obstinate beings for days or weeks . . . or even longer!

So, while you can count on your child's growing and changing in ways that can and *will* challenge you, there is a growth pattern that most kids follow. I recommend that you keep a good child development book around so that you can take an educated guess at what you're dealing with when you're frustrated with your child. If you would like some additional information about child development, the Resources section lists some books that I think you would find helpful.

Using What You Know About Your Child

Children watch and learn from their parents or guardians. What do we learn about *them* in the process? Do we know what their strengths and weaknesses are? What they are afraid of? What they love best?

As your children's most important teacher, you should take advantage of your position to observe them and to gather useful information about them. From day to day and week to week, notice changes; watch how they are growing. It stands to reason that just by being with your children day in and day out, you know more about them than anyone else. I'm going to show you how to take advantage of what you know about your children to effectively teach them personal safety.

Here are some important questions to consider:

1. Do you provide your child with a great deal of freedom, relatively little freedom, or an amount somewhere in between? How well does he handle the privileges and responsibilities you give him?

2. Does your child have good judgment? If so, how does your child demonstrate it?

3. How would you describe your child's ability to communicate? Can she discuss things that trouble her with you or with others?

4. How does your child get along with other children? With other adults? Is she able to assert herself and make her needs known?

5. How would you describe your child's level of self-esteem? Does he feel worthwhile and competent? How do you know?

6. Thinking about your child's ability to problem solve, what are her strengths? What are her weaknesses?

7. What could a stranger or friend offer your child that would seriously tempt him? Is there something your child wants that you cannot or will not purchase?

8. Does your child feel particularly responsible for other people? Is he likely to assist a stranger who appeals for help?

9. Does your child have a strong desire to please adults? Does she have a strong need for others' approval?

These questions will help you establish a baseline for teaching, a starting place for what your child needs to learn. Question 1 helps you evaluate how much freedom or responsibility your children currently have and how well they handle it.

What safety skills your children need largely depends on what you expect of them. Questions 2 and 6 relate to your child's ability to problem solve and use good judgment, functions that develop in grade school. Good judgment—a characteristic that many parents worry about—varies widely among children. Some children don't develop it easily; others seem to adopt a thoughtful and moderate approach to life from infancy on. Questions 3 through 5 deal with communication and self-esteem, two important foundations of personal safety discussed in chapter 3. Questions 7 through 9 assess how vulnerable your child would be to three effective ploys used by molesters and abductors—bribes, affection and approval, and asking for help.

If the answers to these questions didn't come easily, it could be a signal that you need to observe your child more closely—and objectively—to get this important information. It also may mean that your child is too young for you to have the answers to all of these questions quite yet.

Next, you're going to evaluate your child's level of personal-safety preparedness by checking off which statements are true. This personal-safety checklist takes inventory of your child's strengths and identifies his areas of weakness. For our purposes, we'll refer to strengths and weaknesses as *assets* and *liabilities*. I recommend that both parents fill it out separately so that you can compare your assessments.

In the list below, the column titled "Safety Assets" names the skills or characteristics that would keep most children safe. On the other side is a column called "Safety Liabilities," which lists those behaviors that would increase a child's odds of being victimized. For each item, place a check in either the Assets or the Liabilities column. I suggest you do this for each of your children between the ages of three and twelve. Also, don't be put off by the length of this list. It purposely covers most of the personal-safety skills your child—and your preteen—would ever need.

Safety Assets

___Can say no to adults
___Can name all parts of her body, including private parts (genitals)
___Can turn down a dare
___Can recognize and trust his feelings
___Can recognize and say no to uncomfortable touches
___Can follow rules well
___Can talk about problems or feelings
___Will risk making a scene if necessary
___Can use 911 or Operator in an emergency
___Knows name, address, and phone number
___Knows how to safely interact with strangers
___Would refuse a bribe from an adult
___Knows how to answer the phone without disclosing too much information
___Will open the door only with your permission
___Would "Yell, Run, and Tell" if in trouble

___Questions adults' motives and doesn't automatically trust them

Safety Liabilities

___Is compliant with all adults
___Is embarrassed by or cannot talk about her genitals

___Will accept dares
___Ignores or cancels out feelings
___Seeks or accepts affection from most or all adults
___Has trouble following rules
___Has difficulty talking about problems or feelings
___Won't draw attention to herself or ask people for help
___Doesn't know how to call 911 or 0
___Does not know all identifying information
___Is terrified by or very friendly toward strangers
___Would accept a bribe from an adult
___Tells callers too much information

___Opens the door to anyone

___Would freeze and not be able to think or act in an emergency
___Is easily persuaded by adults

Safety Assets (cont.)	Safety Liabilities (cont.)
___Knows what to do if he gets lost or separated from you	___Doesn't know what to do if he gets lost or separated from you
___Can distinguish between uniformed officers and other people who are masquerading as authority figures	___Would obey anyone who was wearing a uniform or flashed a badge
___Would never keep a secret from you, especially those involving an adult	___Would keep a secret if threatened or scared
___Would recognize tricks that sex offenders and abductors use and can resist them	___Could be tricked by someone who gained his trust and confidence

DISCUSSION

Now look over your list. How did your child do? Does he or she have more personal-safety assets than liabilities? Or did you find yourself checking off more items in the liabilities column? This inventory can be an eye-opener. If you realize that your child is more vulnerable than you thought, be sure to read this chapter carefully. I'll show you how to turn those liabilities into assets one by one.

You may have noticed that most of the assets listed are appropriate for children six years of age and over. That's because our primary job with very young children is to protect them and to set the basic foundations for personal safety. As I discussed earlier, the actual grasp of and ability to use most personal-safety information doesn't come until sometime in grade school. So don't expect your preschooler to have the majority of the abilities found under the assets column. If your child is just entering preschool, don't be alarmed if you checked off *only* liabilities; it simply means that he or she is too young to have mastered those skills yet.

Many of us don't really know under what conditions our children would be vulnerable. And if you guess, you risk drawing your conclusions on the basis of incomplete and, perhaps, biased information. Drawing false conclusions can inadvertently put your children in jeopardy.

I suggest the following strategy: Before you place a check mark next to any of the assets on your child's personal-safety inventory, have your child *demonstrate* to you that he or she can respond safely in that particular situation. You'll have peace of mind only when your child shows that he or she can think and act safely in a suspicious or dangerous situation. How your children can demonstrate their personal-safety skills will be discussed in chapter 10.

Also, I suggest that you ask your partner to complete this inventory of personal-safety assets and liabilities—if he or she hasn't already—or ask an adult friend who knows your child well. Let older kids—ages ten through twelve—fill one out, too. Then compare lists and see if you agree on your child's strengths and weaknesses. Although you may know more about your child than anyone else, you may also need feedback in gathering clear and objective information before you begin to teach personal safety.

A Look Inside Their Bag of Tricks

The main weapon pedophiles and most abductors use is deception. Be assured that it is possible to teach your children to recognize and resist seduction and abduction attempts. The prevention strategies I'll give you in chapters 6 through 9 will enable your child to be wise to tricks and ploys so they won't fall prey to offenders who are skilled in using them.

As we discussed in chapter 3, children who have low self-esteem and who are starved for affection are easy targets. The typical molester showers the intended victim with gifts and affection. He tells the child that no one cares more about her than he does. Once she is willing to keep secrets about their "special relationship," the molester initiates sex. Most children have a hard time believing that someone they know and trust would sexually exploit them. Manipulating their victims with bribes, affection, and in some cases threats, molesters ensure that the relationship continues and is kept quiet.

One of the most effective ploys abductors use is to ask children for help. Children who are taught to be helpful, no matter who asks for help, are easy prey. An abductor drives alongside a child walking down the street and asks for help reading a map. Once the child approaches the car and is within reach, the abductor pulls the victim inside and speeds off. Or an abductor pretends to be worried about his lost pet and asks for help in searching for him. The child doesn't recognize the potential danger and follows the abductor into the woods and away from a supervised or public area.

The TV special, "Stranger Danger," illustrated another trick that abductors use. A very official-looking man approached a preteen in a store and flashed his "security badge" at her. He explained that there had been a rash of shoplifting incidents in this particular store, and that although she wasn't being accused of anything, he insisted that she go with him for questioning. The girl complied and went with the imposter.

In another scene from the same television special, a stranger tried to convince a boy that there had been an accident and that he had been sent to bring him to the hospital. First he called the boy by name and identified himself as a friend of the family. (The boy's name was prominently displayed on his backpack, which made it easy for the stranger to pose as a friend.) Then in a very concerned and urgent tone, he told the boy of the accident and insisted that they hurry to the hospital. The boy became so confused and alarmed that he overlooked the possibility that the man wasn't who he said he was. And he didn't have the presence of mind to question whether there really had been an accident. By playing on the boy's emotions and creating a sense of urgency, the abductor succeeded.

Lessons from Sex Offenders

How do we teach our kids to avoid being manipulated and deceived by such conniving criminals? Is it possible to teach them to carefully consider people's motives without making them distrustful of all adults?

Yes, it is. Start by making good use of what we know about sex offenders and abductors. And remember, while it's important for *you* to understand the motives that drive sex offenders to acts of molestation and kidnapping, it is *not* important that your children be given this information, at least not until their adolescence. They will, however, greatly benefit from discussions in which you give them the opportunity to ask questions and clarify information.

One thing we know about sex offenders is that they are more likely to victimize children who play unsupervised or are alone in other public places. Molesters and abductors prowl areas where they are most likely to find kids who are alone or with a few friends, *not* with an adult. So, if your child doesn't fit this profile or you're not allowing her out on the streets without you or another adult, you can postpone talking about how to avoid some of these awhile. But, if you allow your children this kind of freedom now or you plan to soon, it's *essential* that you prepare them for the potential risks that come with more independence.

Another thing we know about molesters is that some of them use their position of authority to force children into sex. A case of molestation involving nine plaintiffs and three priests was reported in the newspapers recently. All of the victims are now adult men who came forward to report sexual abuse committed by their priests in rectories and summer camps twenty years ago. One of the plaintiffs said that at eleven years old, his priest was like "Jesus Christ" to him. "It's hard to tell someone Jesus Christ molested you. Father Gary was God."

And before you decide to let your preteen head out of the door on his own, consider the words of convicted child molester, Ross Nelson, who is now serving a twenty-year sentence in a

Texas prison. For more than forty years, he seduced boys into having sex with him. The following excerpts are from his April 1992 interview with *Redbook* magazine.

> Meeting boys was simpler than you might imagine. I never had to force or intimidate them, or offer them money or other bribes. Most of them came along with me willingly. . . . Most I picked up while riding my motorcycle, cruising city parks, or just parking at a convenience store and waiting. Adolescent boys can't seem to resist a motorcycle.
>
> Boys who had an emotional—rather than economic—need for a friend like me were most easily controlled. . . . I was careful about the boys I went after. I watched for two physical types: early maturers who reach puberty about ten or twelve years old and late bloomers who don't hit puberty until fifteen or so.
>
> I chose him to talk to because he seemed quiet, and he was alone. . . . I head over casually and make a friendly remark about the merchandise. He smiles shyly. He's always been taught not to talk to strangers. But I've smiled and chatted and shown interest in him. I'm not really a stranger anymore . . . I offer to buy him a hamburger or a slice of pizza. He may hesitate. But finally he smiles and agrees. From then on, he's mine.

This account is chilling enough, but then Nelson becomes nostalgic about his relationships with the boys he has seduced over the years:

> I also remember some happy, beautiful times: being the best man at a grown boy's wedding, watching a boy graduate from high school and knowing I'd helped him get there, taking another out to a fancy restaurant when his folks had forgotten his sixteenth birthday.

At the time of Nelson's arrest, large amounts of child pornography were confiscated from his home. He had been convicted once before in 1983, was fined $600 and received three years' probation. In one eight-month period, Nelson counted that he had molested twenty-nine young boys. It was at that point that he realized he had a sexual addiction. However, he continued to molest boys until 1988 when two boys with whom he'd had sex turned him in. His comment about that arrest: "I wasn't angry at the boys—I believe they were coerced."

Molesters are expert at rationalizing their behavior and at being devious and manipulative. But now you know how their minds work. Armed with the information in this chapter, and with the strategies I will present in chapters 6 through 9, you can help your kids stay out of their reach.

CHAPTER 6

What to Teach and When to Teach It

How do you know what safety skills to teach your kids? And, how do you know when the right time is to teach them? Some parents I meet are concerned about teaching their kids too much too soon or, worse yet, too little too late. And others worry that their children will forget crucial information in an emergency.

There is a fairly simple answer to the questions about what to teach and when to teach it. It's a fact that every good teacher knows, a guiding principle in education that we, as parents, can use with our kids. Children learn information or skills *when they're ready to learn them.* In other words, it's your child's ability to grasp information that determines how much learning takes place. No matter what you think your child needs to know, it is your child's learning readiness that must guide you in what you teach. So, before you start teaching your child personal safety, you must ask questions like "What words and ideas will make sense to him?" "What is she likely to *learn* and *remember*?"

To help you teach your children information that they will be able to learn and remember, I've divided the personal-safety information into three age groups: (1) what's appropriate to teach children in preschool and kindergarten, (2) what's appropriate to teach children in grades one through three, and (3) what's appropriate for children in the upper primary grades, four through six.

The three divisions are based on a general range of intellectual and interpersonal skills that children develop within these age groups. Intellectual skills refer to their ability to understand words and concepts and to solve problems. Interpersonal skills refer to their social abilities, including how well they communicate with others.

As you consider your child's learning capacity, consider his social maturity as well. A child's ability to effectively use personal-safety information depends, in part, on his willingness to behave in ways that are sometimes uncomfortable; for example, saying no to an adult or telling you a secret he was told not to tell. These behaviors represent difficult exceptions for young children—as well as for some older children—who have been raised to respect and obey adults.

Also, in order for children to recognize when adults are behaving inappropriately, they must first understand what *appropriate* behavior looks and feels like. Only then do they have an adequate basis for comparison in the event that an adult mistreats them. Think about preschoolers who are just beginning to have relationships with people other than their parents and primary caretakers. It would be extremely difficult for them to recognize or say no to inappropriate adult behavior, especially subtle or manipulative behavior.

Preschoolers, whose worlds are just beginning to include adults outside their families, should be expected to learn only a few safety concepts, like the difference between "OK" and "not OK" touches. Then, as they get older, we can help them grasp that there are some people in the world who don't have children's best interests at heart. But we don't expect them to have the emotional resilience of, say, an eleven-year-old, nor should we teach them facts that would only confuse and upset them.

Children must also be able to identify and trust their feelings. Recognizing and expressing subtle feelings like "uncomfortable" or "confusing" is difficult for a typical five-year-old; it requires more sophisticated emotional skills. In general, while we can set the *foundation* for personal-safety skills when children are in preschool, we must understand that the social maturity to effectively use most personal-safety skills won't come for a few more years.

Be aware that your child's intellectual and interpersonal abilities may not mature at the same rate. For instance, your child's thinking and problem-solving abilities may be at age level, but his social functioning may be a little below age level. (By the way, this unevenness is typical of how most kids grow and is totally normal.) So, when you read the personal-safety information in chapters 7 through 9, and you know or suspect your child is functioning at one level intellectually but at another level socially, read the information about *both* age levels. Ultimately, what's most important is that you select and teach personal-safety information that *your* child can learn and remember. The rule of thumb is to start teaching at the level your child is most likely to understand, *regardless* of what age group he or she is in.

Also, remember that learning is a process that occurs over a long period of time. Children—or adults for that matter—can't learn everything there is to know about personal safety in one sitting. You can't make a list of ten safety rules for your children to follow, post the list on the refrigerator, and consider your job finished. Besides, teaching kids information without giving them the opportunity to practice it is like teaching them how to swim without ever letting them get into the water! Your children learn and remember personal safety by having it repeated, by asking questions and having discussions with you, and by practicing their safety skills. By aligning your expectations—and your approach—with what your children can realistically learn, you're giving them information they will be able to remember and use if the need arises.

Selecting What to Teach Your Child

It's important to teach personal safety according to commonly accepted child development guidelines. To assess what to teach and when to teach it, you must consider your child's age and level of intellectual, emotional, and social maturity. Again, your goal is to teach safety information when your child is most likely to learn and remember it.

As you select what to teach your children, remember to pace the information over time so that your children don't become overwhelmed or confused by too much at once. But kids need to hear about how to manage situations *before* they're likely to encounter them. Here's a good rule: Shortly before you grant children the kind of freedom that will make them potentially vulnerable to a particular trick or tricks, discuss how they can use their street smarts to stay safe. Remember, you don't do that by yelling, "Don't take any rides from strangers!" as they walk out the door, headed to school by themselves for the first time. That simply won't work. Instead, in the weeks and days before you grant them a new privilege or responsibility, discuss some of the ploys that they may encounter and teach them how to avoid them. By combining your understanding of what they can learn and remember with what you now know about their assets and liabilities, you'll be much more successful in teaching the essential information that will protect them.

General Guidelines for Teaching Personal Safety

1. **Teach** your children safety information when they are ready to learn and remember it. Consider their intellectual, emotional, and social maturity in what you expect them to be able to learn and use.

2. **Don't try** to teach too many safety skills at once. You don't want to overwhelm or confuse your child. Teach a little bit at a time over time.

3. **When teaching** personal-safety skills to grade-schoolers, first find out whether they have mastered the preschool skills. The preschool skills are essential building blocks for the grade-school skills.

4. **In reviewing** and reinforcing specific safety concepts, start where your child seems confused or unclear. Review each safety skill periodically.

5. **Keep track** of your goals and your progress.

6. **Anticipate** when your child will need to know or use a specific skill. Begin teaching the information or skill several weeks before your child will need it to allow for adequate practice.

7. **Each child learns** personal-safety skills differently. You will need to spend more time on some skills and less time on others, depending on your child's strengths and weaknesses.

CHAPTER 7

Personal-Safety Skills: Preschool through Kindergarten

Children three to five years old live in the present; they are focused on the here and now. They have no interest in adults' "maybe's" and "we'll see's," which are part of an abstract world of things that *may* or *will* come. Therefore, you may notice that preschoolers are often impatient and unable to wait for something they want. This doesn't mean they weren't listening when you said "maybe later." It simply means that waiting patiently for the future is beyond their ability for now.

Preschoolers of this age also have an impossible time making exceptions and are often confused by general rules like "Don't talk to strangers." According to child development expert Penelope Leach, the first problem with this rule is, What exactly do we mean by the word *talk*? The second problem is, Whom do we mean by "strangers"? Leach says that small children can't make sense of a general rule that forbids them to speak to people they don't know and then encourages them to "speak nicely to the bus driver, say thank you to a storekeeper, and be good for the new babysitter." On top of this, we tell them not to talk to strangers, but they see *us* do it every day! Positive instructions that describe "what they should do—*always*—rather than something they must not do—*usually*" will best protect children, says Leach.

That's why, instead of telling them "Don't talk to strangers," we must give them understandable rules like "Always come and tell the grown-up in charge before you go anywhere with anybody."

Because very young children are so easily deceived, our teaching efforts must include rules that require them to check in with adults continuously. At this stage, the burden to protect our children is on us. In my own family, this rule was firmly established when my daughter was three. We asked her to keep us informed of her whereabouts, even if she was only off to the bathroom. We made it clear that we always wanted to know where she was or where she was going. This made good sense to her because children of this age are extremely interested in where *you* are. Soon, announcing her "travel plans" became a natural part of our conversations. After a while, she did the same thing with her teachers and baby-sitters.

Another developmental factor to consider is that preschoolers have difficulty understanding that a trusted adult might do something harmful to them. In their minds, trusted adults care for them and are good to them.

"They simply cannot conceive that people they and their parents or teachers know as friends might behave as enemies," Leach says. So, we don't attempt to train preschoolers to evaluate the boundaries of appropriate adult behavior. And we don't assume that they are equipped to prevent an assault or abuse. What we *can* teach them to do is to say no to behaviors that are easy for them to understand—like saying no to "bad touches" or to people who want to take them somewhere without their parents' permission. We give them simple rules and we limit their choices, because this is what makes sense to them and fits in with their thinking.

The biggest advantage you have in teaching personal safety to preschoolers and kindergarteners is that they love rules. In fact, they *count* on rules. Have you noticed that when you forget and stray slightly from a rule you've set your child will remind you of it and hold you to it? Most young children enjoy following rules; they particularly enjoy ruling over their playmates with the royal endorsement "My mommy said . . . " I've seen preschoolers remind adult relatives, baby-sitters, and teachers about what the rules are. You can be assured that if you present personal-safety rules just like any other rules—in clear, simple, and nonalarming terms—your children will follow them.

Take advantage of your child's need for consistency. A preschooler will quickly notice when something outside of his normal routine is happening. You want to promote this kind of awareness. A friend's preschool son often returns home with a report about what was "different" on any given school day. The boy talks about who was absent, or about a substitute teacher, or about how the class ate their snack after playground instead of before. The father often replies, "You're a very good noticer!" It's easy to imagine this boy immediately alerting his father if *any* adult acted differently than he had been taught to expect. Good observation skills serve children well by alerting them to unusual or suspicious behavior and should be encouraged.

Obeying Limits

It seems as if we're always setting limits for young children, making sure they don't wander off and insisting that they stay where we can see them. There's a reason for this. Toddlers and preschoolers don't understand what's safe and what's not. So, our role is to *tell* them and *show* them. By providing limits you're ensuring your young child's physical well-being. *This is the beginning of personal safety.*

Your child needs you to take an active role in setting limits. Eventually—although there may be some days when you won't believe this—your child *will* be able to do that for himself. But for now, you must step in and say yes or no. And be sure that you teach your child clear information like "This is safe. That is not."

Naming All Body Parts

At around age three, children can start naming their body parts and can learn which parts are private. This is an important skill. We start when they are in preschool to teach them an unself-conscious language that includes words like *private parts*. We want them to be able to identify and name all parts of their body with comfort. That means that we must teach them to say "penis" as comfortably as they say "elbow," and to say "vagina" as easily as they say "nose." We convey our level of comfort and kids match it, by learning to feel embarrassed or comfortable themselves.

All kids need to be able to identify different parts of their body as part of building their vocabulary and basic awareness. And there's another excellent reason for investing energy in having kids develop "body vocabulary." In the event of a molestation, your child will be able to accurately identify which parts of his body have been abused.

Without hesitation a child should be able to report that "a man was walking around with his penis hanging out" or that "someone tried to touch my vagina." If a child doesn't know the right words or is made to feel that certain parts of the body are unmentionable, there can be no communication about what happened, and parents will be unable to help.

Distinguishing Between "OK" and "Not OK" Touches

Part of helping children understand who is allowed to touch their private parts is to teach them the difference between "OK" and "Not OK" touches. You'll be teaching them how to recognize uncomfortable feelings and what to do if they don't want to be touched. Remember, you're setting the stage for preschoolers to be able to say "NO" to inappropriate touches.

T. Berry Brazelton, M.D., says to assure three- and four-year-olds that their genitals are "their own" and are private. Help them realize that if they don't want older people to touch or handle them they should say so—and even cry out about it. You can certainly teach a child to say, "That's not OK. Let me go!" or "Don't touch me there, those are my private parts."

Examples of "OK" Touches	Examples of "Not OK" Touches
A hug when the child wants one	A hug that is too hard or lasts too long
Holding hands	An unwanted kiss
An arm placed gently around the child's shoulder	Being tickled after the child says "Stop!"
A gentle kiss on the cheek, at bedtime	Hitting, kicking, and punching
Rocking or holding younger children	When a grown-up touches the child's private parts
	When a grown-up forces the child to touch or kiss him or her

Knowing What a Stranger Is

Here's the best definition of a stranger that you can teach to a child younger than five: "A stranger is someone we don't know." Do you hear how simple and nonalarming that is? "A stranger is someone we don't know." Your goal—starting when your child is in preschool—is to teach her to be aware of strangers. Much of what you'll be teaching at this stage is how to distinguish between family, relatives, friends, and strangers. Later on, you'll show her how to distinguish between acquaintances and friends. This is an important distinction every child needs to know how to make, but not one that you can teach a child this young. What's most important at this stage is that you teach your preschooler who's who in her world and to be a good observer of the people around her.

Knowing Identifying Information

It's important to teach your preschooler his full name, address, and phone number. Once he learns this information, help him to overlearn it through repetition. Why? Because overlearning it will help him recall it in an emergency. If someone asks him for his name, address, or phone number at a time when he's upset or afraid, he will still be able to recall it. Be sure to teach your child that if a police officer, firefighter, or telephone operator asks for his name, age, address, and phone number, it's OK to tell these people.

By the way, if your child learns his identifying information but is shy about telling it to anyone except you, this means that for now he would be unable to assist helping people in an emergency. From this you must conclude that he would be at greater risk if he were to become separated from you or lost and should therefore be closely attended. You need to give children who are unable to recall or repeat their identifying information upon request more time and practice.

Dialing 911 and 0

I remember hearing about a parent who taught her young child to use *nine eleven* in an emergency instead of *nine one one*. When there was a fire in their home, the boy was unable to summon help because he kept looking for the number *11* on the phone dial. Ask your preschooler to *show* you that he knows how to dial *911*. Then discuss what an emergency is. There's no guarantee that your preschooler will be able to call for help in an actual emergency, but you can increase your odds for success if you practice how to use 911 on a regular basis.

Stepping In and Speaking Up

At this stage, children are highly trusting. That's why you must be so active in intervening between them and other people.

Remember the example of the stranger who approached a parent and her three-year-old? In that situation the parent stepped in and set personal boundaries on the child's behalf. For kids five and younger, the best protection is being there and being willing to set limits that your child may not yet be able to set for herself.

Exuberant and affectionate preschoolers, many of whom seek hugs and kisses indiscriminately, are more at risk. For those children, physical contact may be their main way of communicating. Affectionate children need to be encouraged to use words to communicate as well. Teach them that words are better than hugs and kisses with people they don't know. Also teach them that adults they don't know, like waitresses, shop clerks, or delivery people, should use words rather than giving them hugs and kisses. At this stage, you can make a simple rule about physical affection being reserved for a few special people in your child's life.

Ask Permission First

Have you told your young children that they must ask permission from you before they accept candy? It's a common rule parents teach, partly because they're trying to limit the sweets their children eat. But, whatever the motives, this rule is a good one because it has excellent personal-safety benefits.

If, early on, you teach your children that they must ask you before they take candy or gifts from anyone you don't know, they will be less vulnerable to molesters or abductors who use this ploy. Tell your child that unless you give your permission, she is not to accept any treats or presents from people outside the family. Of course, you may want to make a few exceptions to that rule and include grandparents or family friends.

I'm encouraged by letters from parents who write to say that their preschoolers now run to them to ask if it's OK to accept the candy from the "nice man" or the "pretty lady." This simple rule adequately protects most preschoolers and should be reinforced periodically with verbal reminders.

No Secrets Allowed

Tell your child, "Adults may not ask children to keep secrets" and "Grown-ups aren't allowed to tell children that something bad will happen to them or to the people they love if they don't keep a secret." In some well-publicized cases, molesters used horrifying images to silence their young victims, such as killing bunnies and kittens in front of them. Then they told the children that they would be next unless they keep the secret. Tell your children that no one may threaten them, and say, "If any adult tries to scare you into keeping a secret, come tell me right away."

Key Points

You can teach most preschoolers to:

- Identify and name all body parts.
- Learn the difference between "OK" and "Not OK" touches.
- Identify strangers and helping people.
- Learn and recite identifying information—name, address, phone number.
- Use 911 or 0 in an emergency.
- Reserve physical affection for family and friends.
- Ask permission before accepting gifts or candies from nonfamily members.
- Tell you if anyone tries to scare them into keeping a secret.

CHAPTER 8

Personal-Safety Skills: Grades One through Three

When I was seven, growing up in a small town in Iowa, my nine-year-old sister and I were walking home for lunch, a four-block walk we had navigated safely hundreds of times. On this particular day, while we were waiting at the corner for the traffic light to change, a group of men on motorcycles rode up to the intersection. In an instant, one of the men swept me off the curb and put me on his bike. I can still remember how he laughed and called out to his friends, "Shall we give her a ride?!" Terrified, I screamed for my sister to go get our mom. My sister ran down the street, the light changed to green, and suddenly I found myself back on the curb. I can still hear the roar of their engines as they rode away, leaving me stunned and shaking on that corner.*

Was this a cruel prank or a failed kidnapping attempt? We never found the man who turned that noontime walk into a frightening and unforgettable childhood memory for me, so I don't know the answer.

Note: Make sure your grade-school child has learned the preschool safety skills discussed in chapter 7 before you teach the skills covered in this chapter.

I share this experience with you because many of you allow your small children to walk to and from school or to the store and back, perhaps believing that it is safe for them to travel with a sibling or a friend around the same age. Consider that at ages nine and seven, respectively, neither my sister nor I had a clue what to do when that man picked me up off the curb. Maybe it was my yelling to my sister to get our mother, who was three blocks away, that made him put me down. Or maybe it was always his intent to put me back down, once he had scared the living daylights out of me. I don't know what it was that helped me return safely to that sidewalk, but I know that after a while—after the meetings with my parents and the school principal and the police—I felt lucky.

Today, I drive or walk my child the three blocks to her school. But if my husband or I couldn't take her, I would either send her with some neighbors who drive their kids each day or hire a responsible neighborhood child—an eleven- or twelve-year-old—to come by for her each morning. One vivid lesson I learned from my own experience is that no small child is any match for an abductor who uses his physical strength to overpower her. And two young children walking together aren't necessarily a safe force against abductors. Sometimes it's as simple as lifting one child off a curb while the other one watches.

If you allow your child to ride his bike to a friend's, to walk to school with a child his age, or to run to the store for you, you must *fully prepare* him with street-smart skills that he can *demonstrate* to you, skills he can remember and use in an emergency. Teach your child to stand back from the curb at crosswalks and to walk on the sidewalk rather than on the grass. Make sure he knows how to yell for help. Something like "Put me down! I don't know you!" or "Help! A stranger is trying to take me!" would draw people's attention. You must base your decision to let your children travel unsupervised—even a short distance—on their demonstrated ability to handle themselves in a dangerous or unsafe situation. Otherwise you are putting them at risk.

I recommend that you use the years between six and nine as a training ground or practice period for your children. Once they have had experience practicing the various safety concepts and skills *under your supervision,* you can begin to let out the reins . . . slowly. I firmly believe in cutting kids some slack when parents have good evidence that they can handle it. Remember, your preteens and teenagers will be safer for all the effort you put into personal safety now.

The Age of Concrete Logic

One day, when my daughter was six, she said to me, "Mommy, I like things with beauty in them." I stopped in my tracks and thought proudly, "What a little poet!" But then she continued with, "I like *Beauty and the Beast, Sleeping Beauty,* and *Black Beauty.*" I smiled and laughed to myself, caught once again in the web of my child's six-year-old logic.

Welcome to the age of concrete thinking. When you're dealing with children who are in the early primary grades, you're likely to have conversations like the one I just described. As adults, we take our ability to use abstract reasoning for granted. But children between the ages of six and nine do not yet have the mental capacity to think the way we do. While children at this stage have increased abilities and can accommodate more complex information than preschoolers, we must remember that they are just *beginning* to develop the ability to solve problems.

Five- and six-year-olds, for example, are still in the process of developing their ability to think, reason, and solve problems. We wouldn't expect them to accurately predict the consequences of their behavior yet. So a hypothetical question like "What might happen if you helped a stranger look for her lost kitten?" might be answered with "We might find the kitten."

A lot of misunderstanding can occur at this age, and the way we use slang and common idioms can complicate matters. For example, several years ago, I was treating a seven-year-old girl in therapy. As we were discussing a problem, without thinking, I said, "Let's put our heads together and find a solution." Suddenly, there she was, about an inch from my face, gently tilting her forehead toward mine until our foreheads met, thus "putting our heads together."

How do we talk to our children, given their concrete way of perceiving the world and their tendency to misconstrue our words? Well, for one thing, we do our best to deliver our message on *their* terms, that is, concretely. By that I mean use simple logic and use words and phrases within their vocabulary. Then check for understanding—and misunderstanding—frequently. Now let's discuss the personal-safety skills that you can teach to most children in the lower primary grades.

Responding Safely When Separated from You

You taught your preschooler that it's OK for her to tell certain adults her name, address, and phone number. You showed her how to recognize "helping people." Now, when she's in grade school, you can teach her to *go* to these helping people if she gets lost and to *stay there* until help arrives. Your goal is to help her develop confidence about approaching cashiers, security officers, or police officers, anyone who can help her locate you in an emergency. In chapter 10, I'll show you how to give your child practice in developing this skill.

Yell, Run, and Tell

In grade school, your child can learn the safety skill called "Yell, Run, and Tell." It's a proven technique for safely getting away from suspicious-acting people or unsafe situations. I will show you how to teach it in chapter 10.

At what point your child needs to learn this skill depends on, as I mentioned earlier, how much freedom she is allowed; for example, if she is out in the neighborhood on her own or at the school playground, or if you allow her on your community's streets. Even if you won't be granting her these kinds of freedoms until she's ten or eleven, there are necessary prerequisite skills that she should develop in the meantime.

Trusting Feelings and Acting in a Self-Protective Way

You taught your preschooler to recognize good and bad touches and to protest if he felt uncomfortable. You continue to listen to his feelings and don't judge or criticize him for having negative emotions, thus sending the important message that all feelings are OK. In the process, you are laying the groundwork for his being able to identify and trust his feelings.

Street-smart kids know how to recognize and respond to their feelings. They immediately hear their "inner alarms" go off. They don't discount them, rationalize them away, or pretend they are imagining things. By helping your child identify and trust his emotions—*all kinds of emotions*—you are enabling him to respond more quickly and protectively in an unsafe or suspicious situation.

Interacting Safely with Strangers

Children at this age should be taught how to interact safely with strangers. In general, they should be cautious and be prepared when they encounter a stranger. Children should be told, for instance, that it is unusual for strangers to approach children, that adults are not supposed to ask children for help, and that they shouldn't allow a stranger to get too close to them. Then your next step is to teach them what to do if a stranger approaches them, or asks for help, or gets too close.

Once again, notice that you aren't telling them that strangers are dangerous; rather, you're teaching them how strangers are *supposed to behave* toward children and what to do if they don't behave in the expected or appropriate ways. Scripts for teaching these self-protective behaviors will be presented in chapter 10.

Stay with a Buddy at All Times

Many parents ask me at what age they can allow their child to play outside by himself. I think there are more important factors than age to consider, like the child's sense of judgment, his ability to use safety skills, and how safe his neighborhood is. In general, I think that the buddy system is the safest approach. There is *relative* safety in numbers. But make sure that your child's buddies can follow safety rules and aren't likely to take unnecessary risks when they're unsupervised. Also, if your child is unable to follow your directions or leaves the yard without permission, then he is not ready to play unsupervised.

Answering the Phone or the Door

Without your help, most grade-schoolers won't know how to respond appropriately to people who ask questions on the phone or at the front door. If you allow your grade-school children to answer the phone or the door, be sure they know what to say to questions like these:

"Are your parents at home?" ("May I ask who's calling?")

"Do you know if your daddy has a stereo or a VCR?" ("You'll have to talk to my father.")

The same caution applies to letting your child open the door. Is she likely to open the door for someone who says they have a special delivery? Or a present for her? She should always get you when a delivery or repair person comes to the door *before* opening it. And any stranger who offers a prize or a present must be screened by you as well.

If your child can't wait until you get to the door to open it, or can't follow your example of first looking out the window and asking "Who is it?" then tell her she'll be allowed to open the door when she's a little older. In the meantime, continue practicing with her so that she'll be able to answer the door safely.

By the way, if you prefer that your child *not* answer the phone or the door, that's your choice. Whether you live in a high-crime area or a relatively safe area, it's not essential that you allow your child to answer the door or the phone. However, you must tell her it's OK to let police officers or firefighters into the house.

Using a Code Word

You can teach grade-schoolers that they're allowed to get into cars with certain people. Make a list of *authorized drivers*—people they're permitted to ride with—and teach your child the names on your list. This list would include family members, baby-sitters, and family friends who the child knows well and who have agreed to pick up your child in the event that you can't. It's important to have a written list and to update and review the list periodically with your children. Be aware, however, that some children may forget or could be persuaded to make an exception and go with an unauthorized driver. That's why having a code word is so important.

For the rare times when you may have to send someone who's not on your authorized drivers' list, your best strategy is to say, "There may be a time when I can't pick you up at school and have to send somebody else. To be really sure that it's someone I want you to go home with, we're going to have a special code word. Any driver who has my permission to take you in his or her car will know what our code word is. So, remember no matter what the driver says, *unless he or she knows the code word*, you don't go in the car."

There is one potential problem to be alert to with kids of this age. Some of them have great difficulty keeping the code word private. Check with your children about once a month to see if they have mentioned it to anyone. If they have shared it, decide on a new code word and encourage your children to keep it within the family.

Some Touches Are Against the Law

Tell your children, "There are some people in the world—although not many—who prefer to have children for friends because they are unable to get sexual pleasure from people their own age. Any adult that tries to use a child for this purpose is breaking the law." Explain that affection between an adult and a child should *never* include undressing, touching or kissing private parts, or having sexual intercourse. Children have the right to say NO to being treated this way. To encourage children to report adults who treat them inappropriately say, "No matter who they are, no matter what they've told you, never keep this kind of behavior a secret. Sexual abuse is a matter for police and parents to handle, not a matter for kids to try to handle on their own."

As parents, there is no need to worry that every adult that expresses a fondness toward your child is a molester. But it is necessary to be watchful of and curious about *any* adult who expresses great interest in your child. Be alert and ask questions to ensure that the relationships your child has with adults—teachers, friends, relatives, youth leaders, clergy, neighbors, and coaches—are wholesome and appropriate. Ask yourself questions like "How much contact is there between this adult and my child?" "Has my child begun to show a preference for this person over his peers?"

Sorry, I Can't Help You

Tell your children that strangers shouldn't approach kids for help. Teach them that they have the right to say no to any adult asking for help, no matter what the request is. Reinforce the message, "Strangers should ask for help from other adults, not children."

Encourage concerned children to help those in need through organized efforts, not on their own. Volunteer efforts, along with your reassurances that people are essentially good, will help your child respond to today's social problems without fear and will help maintain his optimism.

Remember, sometimes the rules we set for children at this concrete intellectual stage backfire. Let's say you tell your daughter she must never go with a stranger who asks for help in finding his lost puppy. A week later, you hear that she helped a neighbor look for his lost rabbit. When you ask her about the rule of not helping adults, the child responds, "You said I couldn't help look for lost puppies, not rabbits!" When stating rules to young grade school children, cover all bases and be extremely concrete.

Power Tricks

Don't be surprised if your children react with disbelief when you tell them that some people misuse their power to trick kids into having sex or to abduct them. Especially if your children have been raised to respect people in authority, the truth can disappoint or upset them. Be sensitive to the fact that at this age kids have a concrete view of the "good guys" and the "bad guys." Reassure them that most people in uniform protect children and would never trick them or hurt them. In chapter 10 I'll show you how to teach your child to distinguish between a legitimate officer and an impostor.

Refusing Bribes

Your child must be taught that what may seem like gifts may also be bribes. Teach kids, "A bribe is different than a present because someone expects something back from you in return." Tell children that some grown-ups might expect sexual favors from children in return for a gift. Help them distinguish between a grown-up who, in return for a present, asks for a kiss on the cheek or a hug and an adult who wants the child to do "special favors" for him because he's been so generous.

Tell kids, "Adults can ask for kisses and hugs and children can decide if they want to give them. But, if adults want you to touch their private parts or try to touch yours because they gave you a present, that's against the law." If that happens, tell your child that he should get out of there right away and tell you.

Remember, lonely or unhappy children are more likely to keep these relationships a secret because they are hungry for the special gifts and the much-needed attention. Some would rather put up with being sexually abused than give up the relationship with perhaps the only adult who truly makes them feel special.

When Strangers Say They Know You

It's very popular these days for kids to have their names displayed on their belongings. Abductors have made good use of this trend. When an adult calls your child by name and pretends to be a friend of the family, your child may drop his defenses and fail to act cautiously, *even though the person looks unfamiliar*. To prevent molesters and kidnappers from tricking your child, label all of your child's belongings on the *inside* and avoid personalized clothing items that display your child's name for all the world to see. Tell your child, "If an adult approaches you, calls you by name and acts very friendly, unless he looks familiar to you, stand back from the person and be ready to run and get help." You're teaching children that no matter what a friendly adult *says*, unless they recognize that adult as a friend, they must use the same caution with him as they would with a stranger.

Let's Keep It a Secret

Tell your child, "Adults should not ask children to keep secrets." Also tell him that "it is against the law for a grown-up to touch or fondle you and then tell you that something bad will happen if you don't keep it a secret." If any adult tells your child to keep a secret, your child should know to come to you at once. Let him know that you will believe him and that you won't be angry with him.

Key Points

You can teach most grade-schoolers to:

- Get into cars only with authorized drivers.
- Use a "code word" in special circumstances.

- Approach authorized people for help in an emergency.
- Identify and trust their "inner alarm" and act protectively.
- Answer the door and telephone safely.
- Interact safely with strangers.
- Turn down and report bribes.
- Say no to unwanted and sexually intimate touches.
- Keep no secrets from you.
- Refuse strangers' requests for help.
- Verify an officer's or guard's status before complying with him.
- "Yell, Run, and Tell" when they are in danger.

CHAPTER 9

Personal-Safety Skills: Grades Four through Six

Some children enter puberty at this age, some won't for a few more years. Physical differences among children at this stage become more pronounced; girls develop more rapidly than boys. Some children may show very few physical changes between ages ten and twelve. Others suddenly leap into adolescence—a function of hormones and an impatient wish to look and act "cool."

While preteens may emulate their music and TV idols, they possess neither the social nor the emotional maturity to handle teenage freedoms. I've heard of twelve-year-olds sneaking off on dates after their parents told them they were too young. I know of physically mature preteen girls who are sexually active. However, at the same time, I know many twelve-year-olds who prefer their buddies and their youth clubs and activities over anything remotely related to the opposite sex.

Many kids will want to increase their time away from the

family as they cultivate new interests and get involved with a wide range of activities. While transportation may prove to be the biggest problem you have with these busy youngsters, their peers may be struggling with different kinds of problems. Problems at school, at home, or both can overwhelm an older child, making him vulnerable to depression, drugs and alcohol, and molestation. To complicate matters, as preteens begin their journey toward a separate identity from their parents, they are often moody and critical. This can lead to emotional turmoil at home: Tempers flare, kids feel misunderstood or unloved, and parents get frustrated.

As you see the signs of approaching adolescence, you may want to run for cover. No matter how you feel about the changes in your child, you can't afford to pull back, because your kids need you more than ever. They need you to make sense of the physical and emotional upheaval that's happening—or will happen soon—and they need help in walking that fine line between childhood and adolescence.

Your ultimate goal is to reach the point where your preteen has all the information and ready-to-use safety skills that will protect her as she spends more time away from home. To ensure that this happens, continue to reinforce all the safety information you have taught her so far. You do that by repeating the information, by having discussions in which you listen for any misinformation or confusion on your preteen's part, and by providing increased—and supervised—opportunities for her to demonstrate how well she remembers and uses specific safety skills. In general, from this point forward your job will be to reinforce what you've already taught her and to prepare her for more independence.

Refer to chapter 8 for a review of the safety skills your child should understand by now. If that information is new to you or your child, then start there. It's essential that your preteen has a good understanding of previous safety skills before you teach him the information covered in this chapter.

Good Judgment and Decision-Making Skills

Preteens regularly make decisions, and some of their choices are better than others. Their good judgment is just starting to develop, and for some parents it comes much too slowly. They become alarmed when their kids want to make independent decisions before they have the judgment to make wise ones.

The difference between what *kids* think they can handle and what *parents* think kids can handle is a source of conflict in many families at this stage. As a parent, you may be uncomfortably aware that there's a gap between your daughter's youthful exuberance and her common sense or that your son's bravado is largely for show, mostly for the benefit of his friends. But as kids start dressing like teenagers and listening to popular music, they want to *be* teenagers. Before you know it you have a twelve-year-old asking for the kind of freedom you weren't expecting to think about for several more years.

How do you deal with your preteen's growing need for independence? There are several ways to meet this challenge. One way is to give your child ongoing practice in making good choices and using sound judgment *before* you expect her to make decisions independently. Start by having her make independent choices in situations where making a bad decision will have a light—not a serious—consequence. Afterward discuss how things turned out and why. In using this approach be sensitive to your child's feelings and take care not to send discouraging messages. You don't want her to think she's incapable of making good decisions as you continue to give her supervised opportunities to develop her problem-solving and decision-making skills.

Another option you have is to arrange some activities that are supervised by another adult, if your child is yearning for independence from you. Joining a team or going to a camp gives your child a sense that he is breaking away from you even though he's still in a supervised environment. Bus trips with his team or a session at a sleep-away camp are medium-size steps toward independence that respect his need to be "on his own."

Sixth Sense Savvy

If you allow your preteens considerable freedom now, be aware of and reinforce two qualities that help independent kids stay safe. One quality is their ability to make the distinction between situations where they must take defensive action immediately and situations where staying alert and prepared is sufficient. The other quality is their willingness to trust and act on their intuition. How do you know if your children have these qualities? Discuss hypothetical situations with them.

Take a typical situation they might encounter on the street. What if they see someone acting suspiciously? How do they make a decision that protects them? First, by trusting their intuition. If their gut tells them something's wrong, *it is*. Second, by being able to tell the difference between a situation that requires an action on their part, like yelling or running away, and one that only requires them to be cautious.

If, at this stage, you are allowing your kids to be out in the neighborhood or at the playground without supervision, their ability to use their sixth sense and take protective action is essential to their safety. Make a point of noticing whenever they make an effort to develop and use these skills. You might say, "You were sharp to see that man standing over there by the bushes" or "I'm glad you trusted your intuition. You were right." These kinds of remarks encourage the specific qualities you want children to develop and use as they become more independent.

And, it's not too soon to reinforce these qualities in small children. Whenever they make a remark that shows the *slightest* bit of sound reasoning, to say, "Good thinking!" Also reinforce their ability to be alert and aware with comments like, "You're a very good noticer."

Updating Stranger Skills

If you allow your preteen to play with friends at the park or playground, or to walk alone in your neighborhood, you need to add some information to what you previously told her about safely interacting with strangers. Tell her to:

1. Stay with her friends and not wander away from her group at the park or playground.
2. Immediately step back from the curb if someone pulls up in a car or starts to follow her. No matter what the driver says, stay ten to twenty feet away from the car.
3. Stay at a safe distance—about three feet away—when passing a stranger on the sidewalk in case the adult makes a grab for her. If she feels uneasy about someone approaching her on the sidewalk, she should walk quickly across the street and be ready to get help.

Street-Smart Safety

If your child is allowed on the streets, there is something you *must* do now if you haven't done it already. It's very simple, although it may make you uneasy, but you can't afford to put it off. Prepare a complete identification kit for each of your children. Include a good recent photo and a complete description. Videotapes, fingerprints taken by a qualified individual, and medical and dental records can all help to identify a recovered child. Keep it in a safe, easily accessible place and hope that you will never need it.

In preparing your children to walk to school or ride their bikes through their neighborhoods, you must walk the neighborhood with them, checking for areas that threaten safety, such as abandoned buildings and areas with bad lighting or tall shrubbery. Make a contract with your children to stay on the designated safe routes and to avoid shortcuts or traveling in isolated areas. This is basic street-smart safety.

There are more skills for your children to learn, skills that will involve their ability to recognize danger and to act protectively. Once children move about on their own, they must be prepared to face some difficult and potentially dangerous situations: threats, taunts, bullies, and, in some places, gangs, drug dealers, and muggers.

Some of the skills you taught them when they were young will need to be updated or expanded. For example, when your son was small you told him to always stay "three giant steps back from the curb." Now that your ten-year-old son can estimate distances, update the safety rule by saying, "Stay at least ten to twenty feet from the door of the car if someone stops to talk to you." Ask him to demonstrate what this distance looks like.

Early on you told your daughter to stay with her friends at all times. Now you tell your preteen why it's important that she not fall back or wander off, that she is more vulnerable apart from her group. You get her agreement that she will not travel alone or use public restrooms alone. You remind her that it is unsafe to linger in the schoolyard after her friends have left. Tell her that when she plays in parks and playgrounds, she must always have playmates who can watch out for her.

Teach your preteens that criminals are expert at spotting kids who look like easy victims. You show them what an "easy mark" looks like and how he walks down the street—daydreaming, counting the cracks in the sidewalk, looking lost, confused, sad, or upset—and then you model how a confident and alert kid walks down the street. You tell them that kids who walk confidently and pay attention to their surroundings are less likely to draw attention to themselves. When you send your children off to school by foot or on public transporation, remind them to never flash money, bus passes, or possessions. They should leave expensive items like jewelry or watches at home, along with any clothing that displays their name in large letters.

These are the essential skills for street-smart kids.

Street-Smart Kids:

- use their eyes and other senses to perceive what is happening around them
- trust their intuition and act on it
- can decide when to run for help and when to be cautious and alert
- are prepared but are not overcautious or afraid
- look for and can recall details
- stay with friends at all times
- know landmarks in their neighborhood
- walk in the middle of the sidewalk and avoid bushes and doorways
- know the location of public phone booths in their area
- know and can locate safe places they can go to if they need help
- call no attention to themselves through their dress or mannerisms
- are swift to contact police in the event of a suspicious incident or a crime
- view fear as a signal to act cautiously, not as a sign of cowardice

---

NAVIGATING PUBLIC TRANSPORTATION SAFELY

If your children rely on the bus or subway they will need specific safety skills. For example, your child must learn his route well and ahead of time, including his exact stop and any transfer points. He should identify landmarks and street names along the way and be able to recall them. Tell your child it is his responsibility to stay aware and observant. Burying his head in a book, wearing headphones, or sleeping are not allowed. Neither is displaying any cash or possessions that may draw attention to him. Encourage him to ride near the driver or conductor. Train him to wait in well-lighted spots or designated off-hour waiting areas. And as always, reinforce your child's ability to trust his instincts; if he feels uncomfortable, he should get away. If accosted by a stranger, remind him to draw attention to the situation so that others can help.

If Your Child Needs Help

Kids traveling on the streets should know the safe places along their school route and in their community. Find out if your community sponsors safe houses or safe havens. If they do, walk or drive through your children's neighborhood and point out the homes and businesses with the designated stickers. These stickers might say SAFE HOME or SAFE HAVEN or SAFE PLACE. Previously, you taught them what a helping person is. Now they should have that information memorized and ready to use in an emergency.

Safe Havens	*Safe People*
Fire station	Neighbor
Police station	Family friend
Homes or businesses with SAFE HAVEN (or similar) stickers in their window	Relative
	Police officer
	Security guard
Grocery store	Other person in uniform
Bank	
Library	
School	

Tell your children that if they are in trouble, safe havens will never turn them away. I added the bank and the grocery store to the list because these businesses often employ security guards. Point the guards out to your children or tell them that in most places they are stationed by the front door.

My rationale for suggesting that you teach your children to approach *anyone* in uniform for help is based on three things:

1. Some adults would be alarmed by rather than responsive to an older child who ran up to them screaming for help. They might suspect that the child is up to no good and try to get away rather than to help.
2. People who wear uniforms in their jobs often perform some service or support function and tend to be oriented to helping others.
3. While your children may be at risk if they don't verify the identification of a person who approaches them, explain that they are in little or no danger when the situation is reversed. It is *highly* unlikely that the uniformed person they grab for help is a child molester or abductor.

DEVELOPING STREET-CRIME STRATEGIES WITH YOUR CHILDREN

What's the best strategy to teach your children to use if someone demands their money or possessions? Police advise handing over money or possessions if you believe your attacker will use force and especially if there is a weapon involved. Stress to your kids that this is wise because the mugger's behavior is irrational and unpredictable. Emphasize that their physical well-being is much more important than stuff that can be replaced.

In teaching your child how to respond when being threatened, consider what your child is *most likely to do*. If you have a child who rarely, if ever, backs down in an argument, teach him that it's OK to fight for his possessions as long as it's an *equal* fight. Teach him how to assess whether or not he has a chance of keeping his belongings and to hand them over when it's too dangerous to resist, for example, when the mugger has a weapon. Kids who are unafraid of getting into a fight should be taught the necessity of sizing up a situation before they dive in with their fists.

Stress to children who are somewhat timid or passive that kids shouldn't automatically hand over their money or possessions when other kids want them. Tell them it's OK to stick up for their possessions with friends or siblings but it's not wise to argue with bigger kids or with a kid who is holding a weapon.

Use "What if . . . ?" questions with your kids to help them visualize themselves acting safely if threatened by a mugger.

Father: What would you do if you were on your way to get some pizza with a friend and three teenage boys asked you for some change?

Zachary: I'd ignore them and keep on walking.

Father: But what if the teenagers followed you and threatened to hurt you if you didn't give them some money?

Zachary: Well that's different. Then, I'd give them my money, get a description of the guys, and report the information to the police.

Today, more parents are training girls to deal with muggers the same way boys do. Both boys and girls must learn that the important thing is for them to learn to assess a situation and respond with safety uppermost in their minds. Later in this chapter I'll cover self-defense classes for both girls and boys. I'll discuss how some self-defense approaches help, while others hinder, our children's safety in threatening situations.

Children need to know some general information about muggers and how they operate. Elementary-school-age children, especially small ones, are often targets. Unfortunately, kids who are just beginning to go to school by themselves are easy prey. Usually muggers take their victims by surprise; frequently, there are two or three against one. They don't play by the rules and want the advantage in every situation.

Whether or not to give children a small amount of additional money to hand over to a mugger if they are confronted is a matter for each individual family to decide, according to educator and author Grace Hechinger. Some parents feel that by doing so they are unnecessarily alarming their children or programming them to give up their possessions to anyone who asks for them. Others question whether a little money will placate a potential mugger or prevent their child from being physically harmed. Crime prevention officers suggest that young children carry enough for their lunch plus some extra change tucked into a shoe, an extra dollar at most. No experts advise giving children more money than they need since that sets them up as easy marks.

Safeguard your children by having them change their route to school and walk with older or bigger friends or siblings. Teach them to stay in a group because attackers usually single out and intimidate individuals. And be careful not to alarm your children about street crime. Tell kids that many of the safety rules they already know will protect them: avoiding shortcuts, staying alert about their surroundings, and going places in groups. Stress that if confronted, your children should immediately size up the situation and be prepared to surrender whatever the mugger is demanding. Safety must be uppermost in their minds. They should get a good description of the suspect and report the information. Also, emphasize that if they see an accident or a mugging, they should not get involved but should call the police or ask another adult to get help.

If Your Child Is Mugged

After you have reported the incident—and even if the mugger is caught—your child may need help to cope with his or her emotions. For boys, the idea that they would ever give way to any threat can be a hard one for them to accept because, more often than for girls, their pride seems to be at stake. In addition to sometimes needing to hold on to a heroic account of the story that makes them look stronger or more macho, many boys struggle with the feeling of humiliation. Some, in an attempt to save face, will fictionalize certain details.

For example, one boy who had forgotten to tuck some backup money in a separate pocket felt humiliated by being "cleaned out." So, he changed the account of what happened, telling his parents that the muggers made him empty *all* of his pockets. The same boy embellished the story to his friends afterward with vivid accounts of how many kids there were, how he stood up to them, and how he tricked them.

Help kids who think they should have fought back to recognize that there is no disgrace in walking away from an unfair fight. Tell them that when they're caught in an unequal situation, winning or losing does not apply and in such a case they are not a timid loser by surrendering whatever the mugger demands. For many kids, surrendering their sense of self-esteem is more of an issue than handing over a watch. Victims often need to express their fantasies of defending themselves to regain their sense of self-esteem. It sometimes helps to point out that some of the stories their friends tell about their mugging experiences may be exaggerated. If they got away without being physically harmed, whatever they did was the "right" thing to do.

Don't minimize or belittle the sense of humiliation or anger your child feels. Comments like "Well, you're just lucky that's all he got" or "What's a pair of high tops compared to your life?!" won't help. Your child is likely to feel upset, scared, and angry. You can help by accepting his feelings and helping him look at being mugged as a crazy and irrational situation rather than a test of his mental or physical prowess. Emphasize that it takes courage to walk away when you think you must stay and fight, even if the odds are stacked against you.

For urban children who face the threat of being mugged daily, proving their cleverness or street sense and saving face with their friends and family may become overly important. Many urban kids don't expect to avoid being mugged. What they want is to save face without getting hurt. It's important to stress to all children, but particularly to teens and preteens, that running away from danger won't make them less "cool" or result in their friends' thinking they are cowardly.

Remind your children that being alert and careful on the street does not mean that they need to be nervous or overcautious. Help them keep a balanced view of the world and make sure that if they are mugged they don't withdraw from everyone or stay inside for more than a couple of days. You don't want to reinforce the mistaken notion that the world is filled with bad kids doing bad things to good kids.

AVOIDING GANGS

Like it or not, gangs are a reality in our cities and some of our smaller communities. In teaching children to avoid confrontations with gangs, tell them to avoid traveling alone, especially in unfamiliar neighborhoods. Help them by mapping out gang territories. (Your local police will have some information that will help you do this.) Neighborhoods that are heavily covered with graffiti indicate gang activity as well. If your child sees a gang, tell him it's important not to draw attention to himself. Teach him to go around the block, return the way he came, or go into a business and call an adult for a ride.

Self-Defense Classes

There are many self-defense classes aimed at kids ages ten to twelve. My personal view of self-defense classes—after observing several—is that a few are excellent, some are OK, and some make promises they can't possibly keep. At their best, self-defense classes reinforce what parents are already teaching in terms of awareness, confidence, and caution. At their worst, self-defense classes substitute for parents' involvement and create little warriors with unrealistic ideas about their physical abilities.

Look for self-defense classes that:

- emphasize prevention rather than aggression
- focus on how to avoid, control, or stop an attacker
- teach children not to put up a fight against a knife or a gun
- promote sixth-sense judgment and critical thinking
- take the children's age and size into account
- use positive, confidence-boosting language

Beware of classes that:

- make claims of quick mastering of skill
- use graphic or violent language
- instill fear by overemphasizing danger
- focus on overpowering or "taking down" the attacker
- market to children as young as three years of age

If you are considering a self-defense class for your children, find out what the instructor's credentials are, talk to other parents whose children have taken the class, and, by all means, observe the class before you make your decision.

In chapter 10 I'll give you simple, practical ways of building personal-safety discussions and practice sessions into your family life. I'm going to show you how to teach personal safety on the run and how to make it fun! I'll also give you a system for tracking your progress as you help your kids become safe, strong, and street-smart.

Key Points

With preteens, it's important to:

- Reinforce the idea that sexual experiences with grown-ups are not good for kids. They are against the law.
- Provide supervised opportunities to build problem-solving and decision-making skills. Praise you preteen's efforts to use good judgment.
- Provide supervision—through group and other semi-independent activities—while your child develops the skills and the maturity to handle unsupervised situations.
- Prepare an identification kit; include a good recent photo of your child.
- Teach your child how to deal with street crime. Evaluate available workshops and classes in your area.
- Teach your child that if someone threatens her or tells her to keep a secret, she should come tell you right away. Reassure her that she will not be punished by either you or the offender if she tells.
- Emphasize that learning and using street-safety skills is a responsibility that comes with the privilege of being allowed more freedom.
- Remind them to use their safety skills.

CHAPTER 10

Effective Teaching Techniques for Busy Parents

Five Steps to Your Child's Safety

As a parent you've been teaching your children important skills from the beginning: how to get dressed, how to use a fork and knife, how to cross the street safely. You've had a teaching role in your child's life all along. If I asked you, for example, "How do you teach a child to brush her teeth?" unless you haven't taught this skill yet, you would probably be able to tell me without any hesitation. Perhaps you would say this:

> First, show her how you brush your own teeth. Then brush her teeth for her. Then, once she gets the hang of it, let her practice while you watch. This might go on for a few weeks or months. Once you know she's doing a good job, let her brush without supervision. Also, you're going to need to remind her to brush almost every time. But after a while you won't have to remind her as often. If she gets a cavity, you'll have to start supervising her again, at least until her checkups improve.

By following these steps, you would undoubtedly be successful in teaching a child how to brush her teeth. In fact, this method of teaching would work with any child who could manage a toothbrush. That's because you are teaching several steps using a natural and logical order. This kind of teaching makes sense to adults and it makes sense to kids.

Now for the good news. Teaching this way works with personal safety, too. The same logic and flow—from one small step to the next—can easily be applied to how you teach your child personal-safety skills.

Below is my five-step model for teaching personal safety, using what we know about how kids learn and remember information.

Protect your children—until they are old enough to learn and use the specific safety information.

Prepare your children—with information and skill-building activities.

Practice each skill with your children—while you supervise them.

Prompt your children—with reminders to use what they have learned.

Preview new situations with your children—in which they may need modified/increased skills and awareness.

The process described above is the same whether you're teaching children how to brush their teeth or how to interact safely with strangers. To prove my point that you teach personal safety the same way you would teach a child any other skill, let's contrast how to teach the skill of safely crossing the street—a common safety skill you've taught or will teach soon—with saying no to candy from strangers. Here's how to apply the five teaching steps to teach your children to stay safe:

When They Cross the Street

Protect: Escort your child across the street while she is too young to learn and remember how to cross safely.

Prepare: Tell your child to look both ways for cars before stepping off the curb; when the light turns green or there are no cars coming, she may walk quickly across the street, being alert for cars that might turn into the crosswalk.

Practice: Go to an intersection with your child; ask her to tell you when it would be safe to cross; practice crossing together while discussing what to be alert for; repeat the practice for several days or weeks, depending on your child's progress.

Prompt: When your child has mastered this skill, whenever she will be crossing a street alone, remind her to use her safe street-crossing skills. Then, after she has been crossing streets safely for a while, remind her less often.

When a Stranger Offers Them Candy

Protect: Be present in situations where your small child may encounter a stranger; provide adult supervision at all times.

Prepare: Tell your child that he must ask you for permission before accepting candy from someone he doesn't know.

Practice: Role-play with your child; pretend to be different strangers offering candy; have your child practice saying no and telling the strangers he must ask permission before he can accept the candy.

Prompt: Remind your child to ask an adult before he accepts candy from strangers. If you observe him not following this rule, provide more practice and supervision until he can consistently respond safely to offers of candy.

When They Cross the Street (cont.)	*When a Stranger Offers Them Candy (cont.)*
Preview: If your child will be crossing busy streets or interpreting new traffic lights or signals without you, prepare her with information and/or supervised practice beforehand.	Preview: If your child will be playing at the park or playground, or going to any public place without supervision, discuss how he should respond to adults who approach him or offer him candy (or anything else).

By comparing the two examples, you see that the five steps for teaching your child to cross the street safely also apply to teaching your child to refuse offers of candy from strangers. The process is the same for both skills. Some parents may have a hard time with this concept emotionally. They say, "How can you teach both skills the same way? Being able to get away from an abductor is more important than being able to brush your teeth!" I agree. No doubt you do, too. You would gladly pay for a few fillings rather than see your child harmed or killed. However, while you may *feel* differently about teaching personal-safety skills than you do about teaching more general skills, I assure you that the same positive, patient approach can be used to teach both. And, as we discussed in chapter 4, the more matter-of-fact you are, the more effective you will be.

So, think of teaching safety as a positive and manageable process. First, you wait until children are ready to learn a particular safety skill before you teach it; in the meantime, you provide them with constant supervision. Second, once they are ready to learn the safety information, discuss it with them. Use age-appropriate words and concepts they can understand and answer any questions that come up. Third, provide them with practice activities that help them develop their skill and awareness. Fourth, reinforce what they've learned and review it—frequently, at first. And fifth, anticipate and discuss new situations with your children where they will need to use that particular safety skill. Before you grant a new privilege or freedom, be sure to discuss several hypothetical situations that would require your child to use the safety skill effectively.

Whether you're preparing your son to walk to school alone or you're teaching him to ride his bike, the steps are the same. And while the two skills are fundamentally different, if you teach them in the same encouraging, patient, and calm manner, your child will learn them more easily.

Teachable Moments

Setting up a good time and place for your teaching discussions is important. A heart-to-heart talk about obeying rules can have a totally different outcome if pursued in a quiet and relaxed time period rather than while you're preparing to rush off to the office. In general, when you have important ideas to convey, pick a time when:

- You and your child are both clear-headed.
- There are no distractions.
- Neither of you is too tired to talk.
- Your child is ready to listen or to talk.
- You are not feeling anxious, sad, or angry.

In the space below, jot down the best times and best places for you and your children to talk.

Best Times _____

_____

_____

_____

Best Places _____

_____

_____

_____

If this exercise proved to be difficult, let me share how I found some additional "best times and places" for parents to talk with their kids. Before I became a parent, I noticed many women driving station wagons around town having highly animated conversations—sometimes even laughing—*all by themselves*. Although there was no one in the car with them, they seemed to be having a great time.

This puzzled me. Why were so many women in station wagons behaving this way? What made these seemingly normal women talk to themselves?

Well, those questions remained unanswered until I looked through the windshield of an approaching station wagon one day and saw something I'd never noticed before: just below my line of vision was a *small child* in a car seat. I looked more closely and saw two more in the backseat!

That parent was talking to her *kids,* not to herself! Of course! She and thousands of other parents use the time in the car to talk and play with their kids. They make the most of their errands, car pools, and commutes and create their own "best times and best places" while on the go. What a practical and creative idea!

As busy parents, it's hard to find moments of absolute peace and quiet during which we can devote our undivided attention to our children. Much of the time we are trying to do three things at once. Our constant mental and physical juggling isn't the exception, it's the rule for most of us. That's why we must find alternative ways of connecting with our children—in addition to the quiet times we can create—that fit naturally into our routines.

In speaking around the country, I've met a growing number of parents who are becoming highly resourceful about finding "quality time" with their kids. They approach parenting with flexibility, creativity, and gentle humor. Add a dose of forgiveness and you've got the antidote to the unrealistic expectations and nagging sense of guilt that plague parents in the nineties.

I'm not suggesting, by any means, that we shirk our responsibilities. What I am suggesting is that we take our jobs seriously but take ourselves a little more lightly. This means being more playful, flexible, and creative in *how* we get the job of parenting done.

After considering how hard it would be for most parents to add personal safety to their already long to-do lists, I came to the following conclusion: If we approach teaching personal safety (or anything else of importance) with a positive attitude and a flexible approach, we'll be more likely to teach our children well. I share credit for the idea of teachable moments with all those moms in station wagons who were already putting the idea into practice long before I thought of writing about it.

How to Make Your Job Easier

The key to finding the time to teach personal safety is to look for and use teachable moments throughout your day. In this section, I'll give you some examples of teachable moments that can make your job easier and make the most of your normal routines.

USING TELEVISION TO TEACH

Since it's likely television is a part of your family's life, here are three examples of ways to turn TV viewing into highly productive teachable moments. To start, here's how a Kansas City parent made good use of a program she happened to be watching with her preschooler:

My four-year-old daughter and I were watching a television program together, a comedy. One of the characters addressed a soldier as "Private Parts" and my daughter got the giggles. I took advantage of her interest and began a discussion about her private parts. When I asked her which parts of hers were private, she named them for me easily. "Fine," I thought. Then, I asked her,

"And, who's allowed to touch your private parts?" She said she didn't know. So, I reminded her that she could, that Mommy and Daddy could, and that the doctor could. Then, she said, "Well, people have to wash their hands first." "That's probably a good idea," I said, "but just because a person's hands are clean doesn't mean he can touch your private parts." My daughter started to argue with me, insisting that as long as people's hands were clean, it was OK to let them touch her private parts. At that point I dropped the subject to avoid an argument but made a note that we had some work to do.

This teachable moment—triggered by a comment on a TV program—prompted the mother to review the concept of "private parts" with her child. The parent found out that her child had learned something, but it wasn't exactly what she was trying to teach her. The daughter, with her four-year-old logic and conscientiousness about hygiene, placed more importance on touching hands being *clean* than she did on *what* they touched. Seeing that her child didn't fully understand the concept of private parts, the mother wisely decided to spend some more time on this safety rule.

While the mother certainly made the most of this situation, she also acknowledged that the overall content of the program was not appropriate for her preschooler. If you allow your children to watch adult programming, the kinds of questions you may be asked—and will need to answer—are likely to be more sophisticated. Younger children simply do not benefit from and are often confused by too much information too soon. Limit the amount of time you watch adult programming while young children are around. As I said in chapter 4, you may need to watch the evening news after your youngsters are in bed. The same goes for programs aimed at "mature viewers."

The next example deals with kids' shows and cartoons. I had a hunch that Saturday-morning kids' shows would be a great source for personal-safety material. So, one morning I sat down with my daughter and watched cartoons with her, looking for opportunities to pick up on cartoon characters' safety-conscious behavior—or lack of it. Cuddling together on the sofa, we enjoyed each other's company and I did my research at the same time. (By the way, I'm sure there are plenty of things you would rather do than watch cartoons, but watching a few kids' shows together is an easy way to earn points for spending time with your kids and to talk about safety concepts at the same time.)

The first thing I learned is that kids don't want to talk during their shows. The second thing I learned is that they like the commercials just as much as the cartoons, so the opportunities to make comments are relatively few and far between. But I was able to carve out two teachable moments during the half-hour program: I made a comment when a character made a safe choice and when someone tricked the character into taking unnecessary risks.

As it turns out, cartoons and kids' shows are filled with personal-safety material. Characters continuously make bad choices, trust the wrong people, and get into trouble. Using any number of situations that are presented in a typical half-hour program, there are endless combinations of questions to ask: "Why do you think he did that?" or "How did she get in so much trouble?" or "Do you think he should have trusted that guy?" Then, after your child answers, you can ask another question or review safety information that relates to that character's behavior.

The other kinds of programs that can provide you with teachable moments are safety specials. There are basically two kinds of TV specials, those aimed at kids and/or families and those aimed at adults. For example, a good family special to watch is "How to Raise a Street-Smart Child." It's geared to grade-school children and their parents and airs on HBO once or twice a year. On the other hand, *Something About Amelia*, a made-for-TV movie starring Ted Danson as an incestuous father, is not a show I would recommend for all grade-school children.

If you're curious about a program, I recommend that you tape it and screen it privately. Then, if you feel it would be appropriate for your children, schedule a time for your family to watch and discuss it. Another program I mentioned earlier that airs on the Nickelodeon Channel is called "Stranger Danger." The content is excellent for kids age six and older. Here's a great family program that is filled with enough teachable moments for a month!

In general, it's wise to get information about all safety programs before you allow your children to watch them. Some programs are geared to adults and contain alarming statistics and graphic reenactments. Remember, safety programs for your children should be:

- moderate in their use of explicit graphic images
- reassuring in tone
- focused on specific information that your children can use to stay safe

ERRANDS AND OUTINGS

Think of your child's world as his teaching laboratory. Everywhere you go—to the grocery store, to the bank, to the park—there are people and situations you can notice *out loud and on purpose.* So much of taking advantage of teachable moments simply involves making an observation and listening for your child's response. Sometimes what your child says will lead naturally to another question or a lengthy discussion. Other times, his response will tell you that a personal-safety point needs clarification or practice.

How do you spot these teachable moments when you're out and about? Just be aware of your surroundings. Notice what you always notice, except talk about it *more.* For example, if you spot a house under construction, ask yourself, "Is this something to talk to my child about? What safety issues might be worth reinforcing?" Then say to your child, "Did you notice that new house being built down the block?" And then, during the conversation, reinforce the rule that "you aren't allowed in areas under construction, even if a workman invites you to come in and have a look around."

Here's another common one. Driving through the neighborhood, you might say, "Looks like they've posted a KEEP OUT sign on that neighbor's backyard. Don't you cut through his yard sometimes?" You can easily imagine this comment leading to a discussion about safe routes to and from home.

Or, let's say you're walking down the street with your preschooler. Point out a person walking down the street and ask, "Is that someone we know or is that a stranger?" This ten-second interaction helps your young child distinguish between family and friends and people she doesn't know, a prerequisite to teaching her how to interact safely with strangers.

Learning Activities

As we've discussed, the best way to guarantee learning is to teach children what they're ready to learn *when* they're ready to learn it. The second most important thing is to keep children motivated and interested by *making learning fun.*

The more I meet kids who have been raised on television, videos, MTV, and action films, the more I'm convinced that being earnest and sincere in our efforts is not enough. In teaching personal safety, we must also be willing to use our imaginations and to be at least a *little* entertaining.

Being a playful and creative parent has several benefits. For one thing, it lifts you out of your structured role. When you and your child are being playful, you transcend the traditional parent-child relationship and connect as two people. These can be very intimate times. Some of my best childhood memories are of my father being silly. I can still remember how he used nonsense language to make us laugh and how close I felt to him at those times.

Even if you are somewhat reserved and have strong ideas of how parents are supposed to behave, the ability to play with your child and shed your parental persona for a while has great positive benefits. In my work with children and parents over the years, I've found that three things help adults relate well to kids: honesty, humor, and imagination. When combined, these elements make your child want to listen to you. When applied, they will help you teach personal-safety information in a way that grabs your kids' attention and helps them remember it.

The key to developing successful learning activities is to start with something that both you and your child enjoy. Another important consideration is that learning activities should take very little preparation. In other words, keep them practical and simple. Here are some ways to combine enjoyable things you are already doing with your kids with teaching personal safety.

USING STORIES

If your children enjoy books, read safety stories together during regular story times. Remember, your preschooler won't retain a lot of information at once, so repeat the story or read a few pages at a time. Also, no book is enough on its own. It's a good foundation for teaching skills, but it's just the first step. Once your children understand the ideas in the book, the next step is to turn them into a safety-skills practice.

Another effective approach is to make up a story about safety with your child as the main character. Or, you can take a fairy tale like "Little Red Riding Hood" and retell it so that the little girl uses good safety skills.

Parent: So, when Little Red Riding Hood gets close to the bed, she sees that her grandmother has big, sharp teeth. She thinks to herself, "My grandmother usually doesn't look like this. She says she's my grandma, and she's in my grandma's bed, but I think something's wrong. I'd better get out of here and go get some help."

"The Three Little Pigs" is another fairy tale that can be retold so that all three pigs act safely. It's a good story for teaching kids how to answer the door, because the wolf tries to trick the pigs into letting him in. You could playact the story: Pretend to be the wolf or another person who tries to trick your child into opening the front door.

Think about the safety message in "Snow White and the Seven Dwarfs." You and your child could discuss how Snow White broke an important rule when she took the red apple from the stranger. Most well-known fairy tales contain at least one personal-safety concept you can discuss or role-play. Be creative and look for opportunities to put your child's best-loved books to work for you!

There are many picture and activity books available to use as teaching tools with your children. When selecting a children's book (or audiotape) on personal safety, consider the following:

1. Do you feel comfortable with the approach?
2. Does it seem right for your child's age?
3. Does it emphasize self-confidence and good judgment?
4. Does it give your child specific strategies for staying safe?
5. Are all of the concepts in the book likely to increase your child's understanding?
6. Are there any words or concepts that may instill fear or cause confusion?
7. If there are any alarming or confusing concepts in the book, how would you present them in a way that is helpful and reassuring?

Check the Resources section of this book for recommended books and audiotapes about personal safety to share with your children.

VIDEOS AND TELEVISION

In the previous section, I reviewed what to look for in quality safety programs for your kids. If you decide to use videotapes or

TV programs to teach personal safety, remember that these are only tools for opening up discussion. They won't be effective without your involvement. You'll still need to have a conversation to find out what your child understands.

Parent: Alex, after we watch this video together, let's talk. The program has some good ideas about how to be alert and aware when you go places by yourself. I know you're interested in going out more now, so I think we should talk about what kinds of safety skills you'll need to handle that kind of freedom.

USING THE NEWS

I encourage you to monitor everything your children watch on television. And, if you restrict your children from watching the news, stay alert to the information they get during the commercial breaks. Frequently, during a fifteen-second commercial spot, newscasters come on to announce the "hot" stories for the upcoming news hour. Like it or not, they often do this with sensational language to draw in viewers, often showing the most graphic footage to get your attention.

So, even if you don't allow your children to watch the news yet, there's a good chance they will be exposed to violent or tragic news stories in the course of an evening in front of the television. When you and your children happen to hear about a child's abduction or murder this way, initiate a discussion about it. You might say, "These kinds of news stories really bother me. How about you?" And if a news story doesn't include helpful or reassuring information, take the lead in turning it into a teachable moment that does.

Be prepared for your children's questions. Here's where having the news on late in the evening and storing your newspapers and magazines away from small children's curious eyes can make a difference. If your small son approaches you and asks, "Daddy, what does 'mutilate' mean?" you certainly want to ask where and how he heard the word. More than likely, you'll discover he overheard it on the news. Also, you'll quickly realize what a formidable challenge it is to describe "mutilation" in a way that can be reassuring to a six-year-old. It's a much better idea to be vigilant about protecting your children from explicit or graphic images in the newspaper and on television.

"WHAT IF . . . ?" CONVERSATIONS

If you ask a typical five-year-old to solve a problem, very often her answers won't make sense. But if you ask an eight-year-old to solve the same problem, you're likely to get a reasonable answer. That's because the ability to solve problems begins in grade school. Asking "What if . . . ?" questions is an excellent way of helping your child develop critical thinking skills. In the process, you get instant information about how your child would most likely respond in a given situation. In chapter 4, remember how Eric's mother used this approach to talk about the hypothetical stranger who took her son's bicycle?

Mother: But *what if* this stranger told you he was thinking of getting a bike like yours for his son and just wanted to look at it. Then he asks you to come over and explain something to him.

Eric: Well, since he's just looking at my bike because he wants to buy one, I'd probably go over and talk with him.

By asking the "What if . . . ?" question, the mother learned that Eric was unclear about dealing with strangers. That allowed her to correct the faulty logic he was using and help protect him from this ploy.

"What if . . . ?" questions are also effective in checking for when your child might make unsafe exceptions. For example, many young children know not to enter a neighbor's home if invited in for candy, but if that same neighbor asked them in to watch a video, they might make an exception to the rule. Why? Because, as we discussed in chapter 8, young children think in very concrete terms. And, in many young children's minds, saying no to candy has absolutely nothing to do with saying no to watching a video. That's why you must make *umbrella* rules like "You must always get my permission before you accept treats or invitations from adults."

With all "What if . . . ?" discussions, keep asking questions until your child's answers indicate that she fully understands. If she seems confused or gives you an unclear answer, then you've identified an area where she is vulnerable. Don't panic. Use this as a sign that more information and practice are needed before you expose her to that type of situation.

Here are some examples of "What if . . . ?" questions:

- What would you do if I were late picking you up?
- What would you do if someone tried to touch your private parts?
- What would you do if someone you didn't know started following you or asking you a lot of questions?
- What would you do if someone came to the door with a big box and said they had a present for you?
- What would you do if a fire broke out in our house?
- What would you do if you got separated from me at the store?
- What would you do if your friend dared you to take a shortcut?
- What would you do if an adult told you it was OK to be doing something but you felt uncomfortable?
- What would you do if someone told you they knew your family's code word but had forgotten it?

USING DOLLS AND PUPPETS

Another method of teaching young children personal-safety concepts is to use dolls and puppets. For example, you and your child could make up a story in which the puppets act out a safety rule. Have your puppet model *both* kinds of behavior. In one puppet show, for example, your puppet might obey the safety rule, but in the next show, he might not. Let your child be spontaneous about what his puppet does or says. Very often, if your child sees your puppet making a mistake, he'll try to be helpful and will step in to help your puppet. This is fine. Just be sure to ask your child what he is doing and why. Also, give your child a chance to be the puppet who breaks the safety rule, after he learns it the right way. He'll enjoy pretending that he doesn't know what to do. Then, afterward, give him the chance to show you that he does. In a later section, I'll give you three different safety scenarios to act out with puppets.

SONGS, SLOGANS, RHYMES, AND PUNS

Singing and rhyming work well with your preschoolers. You can teach them a variety of safety information by making the words fun to say or sing. Of course, one of the best things about teaching information this way is that it fits into your other routines. You can sing or rhyme with your child while you're in the car, while you're getting dressed, or while she's swinging on the swing set.

Grade-schoolers, on the other hand, like puns and slogans and slang. When selecting your family code word, let your grade-schooler make the choice if possible. It may not be the most genteel phrase, but be assured he's going to remember it. For one family I know with two preteens, you must be prepared to use the code "That sucks!" if you are an authorized driver sent to pick them up.

USING RELEVANT EXAMPLES

Take advantage of your grade-schooler's ability to use examples to learn personal safety. Telling a related story allows your child to draw direct parallels between the child in the example and herself. And children can't resist solving other children's problems. Whatever the source you use for your example— newspaper articles, friends, other parents—it's essential that the story strike a familiar chord with your child and allow her to solve the problem right along with the character in the story.

Here's an example of a story you could use that would help your child deal with peer pressure. In this story, the girl must make the decision to follow her friend on a forbidden path or stay on the safe route.

Parent: Two girls, about your age, always took their safety route home from school. But, one day, one of the girls, Danielle, dared the other girl, Emily, to take a shortcut home. Emily didn't know what to do. She felt confused because she was supposed to stick with Danielle, but Danielle was going to take a shortcut. And to make things worse, Danielle called Emily a chicken. What do you think Emily did?

DRAWING AND PAINTING

In one of my workshops, I carried this theme one step further. I asked parents to go home and tell the story of Emily and Danielle to their children. But this time, instead of just telling the story, I asked them to add a new medium: art. Here's what two parents came up with, using the same medium but slightly different methods. (In the first example, boys' names are used.)

Parent #1: My nine-year-old son made pictures about this story as we talked. We discussed how Jason felt a lot of pressure to take the shortcut with his friend Scott. My son decided that although it would be hard, Jason should refuse Scott's dare and should stay on the safe route. In the last picture, I asked my son to draw a picture of himself standing next to Jason. I think that left him with a positive image of himself handling the situation well. We hung the picture in his room as a reminder of his ability to make good choices and turn down dangerous dares.

Parent #2: My daughter drew a safety route of her trip to and from school and posted it by the front door. She put orange stickers all along the route to mark safety checkpoints. We used "What if . . . ?" questions to discuss what she would do if a friend dared her to take another way home. She consistently answered that she would stay on the safe route. I felt relieved.

TEACHING TIPS FOR PRESCHOOLERS

Play and imagination are the best tools small children have for learning. Play is their form of work. Let them play and fantasize what you're trying to teach.

It's too soon to expect a preschooler to come up with safe solutions on his own. Suggest ideas for how he could respond safely in different situations.

Keep your activities or discussion short and simple. If you notice your child becoming restless or bored, change the activity or come back to it later.

Preschoolers need to hear and practice new safety information many times. Fortunately, they enjoy repetition. State and restate the information, demonstrate it, and have your preschooler demonstrate it. Practice and repeat until your child overlearns the safety information and will be able to use it in an emergency.

Avoid exceptions to safety rules because preschoolers have difficulty understanding them and will begin to design their own exceptions using naive logic.

Linking Activities with Specific Safety Skills

In this section, I'm going to link various modes and methods for teaching safety with the specific safety skills we've been talking about. As always, your goal is to use teachable moments wherever you find them. Also, think about learning activities in the same way you think about fire or earthquake drills: You do them

TEACHING TIPS FOR GRADE-SCHOOL CHILDREN

Grade-school children are beginning to develop the ability to solve problems. Create "What if . . . ?" situations and encourage them to think out loud with you. You'll quickly learn how well they can use critical thinking and good judgment.

Design safety exercises that include the following steps:

1. Define the problem.
2. Develop alternative solutions.
3. Choose the best solution.

Use a variety of materials and activities. Repetition with grade-schoolers must be balanced with interesting and new approaches.

Use relevant examples to introduce new information. Situations or events that they can apply to themselves are the most effective.

Help them imagine themselves acting safely. Mental pictures of themselves handling safety situations effectively are easier to remember than safety facts and information.

because your child will be well prepared and more likely to stay safe if the real thing ever happens.

Here are some general guidelines for choosing a learning activity:

- The activity should take no more than fifteen minutes unless you are watching a safety program on television or videotape.
- Use materials that are inexpensive or easy to find around the house.
- Keep the learning activity practical and simple.

Remember that preschoolers and grade-schoolers don't necessarily enjoy the same learning activities. What intrigues a seven-year-old is unlikely to interest your twelve-year-old. Because you're teaching safety skills over time, it's important to modify and update your approach to keep up with your child's changing needs and interests. Be flexible and tuned in to what motivates your kids. As they get older and begin to lose interest in learning activities, shift into "What if . . . ?" discussions. By the time they're asking for more independence, your main job will be to review and update safety information and skills.

NAMING AND IDENTIFYING PARTS OF THE BODY

One of the easiest ways to teach your child to name the different parts of his body is during bathtime. Bathtime has many built-in teachable moments. For example, when you're drying off your child, you have a natural opportunity to ask him to tell you the names of different parts of his body and to identify which parts are private. Private parts can be introduced along with the concept of "private property." In both cases, "Keep Out" or "Keep Off" apply, except for a few authorized adults.

Here's one way you can turn bathtime into a learning activity:

Parent: Hey, let's play a game. Let's see how many parts of your body we can name while I dry you off. We'll start with your head and go all the way to your toes!

When you come to parts of the body that you want them to understand are private, you can say:

Parent: If anyone wants to touch you here, you tell them, "I have to ask my mommy or daddy for permission before I let you touch my private parts." Then you come tell us about it right away.

Convicted child molesters say that they have great difficulty molesting children who talk openly with their parents. Based on this information, I tell parents of young children to teach them to say the following words if anyone wants to touch their private parts: "I have to ask permission from my mommy and daddy before I let you touch my private parts." Coming from a small child, this statement is likely to stop most adults in their tracks. It sends out a clear message that the child has been taught to tell and that his parents are ready to listen and to believe him.

Dr. T. Berry Brazelton, a respected and respectful pediatrician, always asks preschoolers for their permission before examining them. Also, he doesn't ask them to take their underpants completely off; instead, he says, "That part of your body is special and you might like to keep it covered."

Do you ask your children if you can undress them or wash their private parts? Does your pediatrician ask for permission before examining your child? Modeling appropriate behavior is very important.

SAYING NO TO UNWANTED TOUCHES

Even parents should not snatch kisses and hugs from their children, says Penelope Leach, nor should they let anyone else do so. If you've been teaching your child from the beginning that adults need to ask permission before hugging or kissing her, she is more likely to protest if someone doesn't ask beforehand.

Teach your child to say, "I don't want a kiss right now" and "I don't want to sit on your lap." Role-play situations so that your child gains practice setting limits with adults. Be sure to act hurt when your child turns you down. After all, this is likely to be the response from some of your family or friends. If they are bothered by your child's reluctance to receive their affection, pull them aside and tell them that you are teaching your child how to say no to unwanted touches. In the meantime, you might suggest that your small children blow kisses to or shake hands with adults.

IDENTIFYING "OK" AND "NOT OK" TOUCHES

You'll need to demonstrate and discuss "OK" and "Not OK" touches with your preschooler. For "OK" touches, you could show two dolls or puppets hugging each other. Talk about petting an animal, another example of an OK touch. Explain that "Not OK" touches hurt, and use examples like hitting, kicking, or pushing. You may want to demonstrate "OK" and "Not OK" touches with anatomically correct dolls. As you do, ask your child, "Is this an 'OK' touch or a 'Not OK' touch? Why?"

Some "Not OK" touches are fairly subtle experiences that not all preschoolers will be able to recognize. Tell the child that sometimes a touch might feel OK in the beginning, but then it changes into a "Not OK" touch. Describe how it feels to be tickled too long or hugged too hard, or to have someone sit too close to you as examples of "Not OK" touches. Then remind them that no one is allowed to touch them in a way that hurts or is uncomfortable, and if that happens, they should tell you.

If this is the first time you've talked about molestation with your grade-school child, you might say: "There are some people who may want to touch your body in ways you don't like. They may try to touch your private parts (penis, vagina, breasts, butt) or have you touch their bodies. You have the right to tell *any* person not to touch you in a way that feels bad or uncomfortable. Even if it sort of feels good, it's against the law for an adult to treat a child that way. Please tell me about it. I will believe you."

Then open the discussion up with questions like "Have you heard the words 'child molester'? What do you think molesters look like?" or "I know it's hard to imagine that an adult you know and like might behave that way, but sometimes even people we care about have big problems. Could you come to me even if the person who took advantage of you was someone you know? Even if they threatened you or told you to keep it a secret?" Encourage him to be honest and open with you, no matter how terrible a secret may seem.

MEMORIZING IDENTIFYING INFORMATION

The best time to start teaching your child her name, address, and phone number is as soon as your preschooler is interested in songs and rhymes. Use songs and rhymes to teach this information because it makes it easy and fun for your child to learn it. Here's a rap song a mother made up for her four-year-old son. I've made a few revisions to protect their privacy.

Mother: Here's a game to say your name
Billy: My name is Billy Williams
Mother: Use the phone to call our home
Billy: 555-800-1234
Mother: Give the address where we live
Billy: 403 Safe Avenue, Denver, Colorado
Mother: With helping people do not fear
Billy: To give my name, loud and clear
Mother: One more time, as strong as you can
Billy: I'm Billy Williams, that's who I am!

HOW TO DIAL 911 AND 0

Do your children know how to use a public phone? Do they know there is no charge for calling the operator or for dialing 911? When your child is small, have him practice calling for help on a play phone. Then graduate to your family phone. With your child listening, call your operator and ask, "What kinds of questions should my child be able to answer if he calls you for help?" I've discovered that having a brief conversation with a "real operator" makes a lasting impression on kids. It also makes the process of calling for help less intimidating. You or a friend can then pose as the operator and have your child call for help.

Teach your children to:

- Speak slowly and carefully
- Give their name and address
- Explain the problem
- Stay on the line until the police operator tells them to hang up

IDENTIFYING HELPING PEOPLE

Who are the "helping people" in your child's world? Just as you helped her identify strangers, you must also point out the people she could approach for help. Remember to teach your child that it is *not* dangerous for her to approach a helping person. However, when an adult who claims to be in authority approaches her, she must always verify his identity.

Here's an example of a learning activity you could use with a preschooler:

Parent: Let's play a game. I'll be a police officer and you be the child. First, I'll ask you some questions and you try to answer them. Then, we'll switch, and you can wear the police hat and ask me questions.

By role-playing, you give your child practice in telling helping people his name, address, and phone number in an emergency. You could also pretend to be a firefighter, an ambulance driver, a security officer, a store cashier, or any person you want your child to identify as a helping adult.

If your child enjoys arts and crafts, you can make pictures about helping people. You can suggest, "How about we make pictures of the different kinds of people that would come to our house to help us? We could draw a police car with police officers in it, firefighters in a fire truck, and an ambulance driver in an ambulance."

What to Do if Separated from You

Explain to your children that if they are in a store and cannot find you, they should go to the nearest cash register and ask an adult wearing a name tag for help. Emphasize that they should stay right there and not wander off. If they are at the zoo or a large public event, they should go to a police officer or to the lost-and-found booth. (Be sure to point out the location of the lost-and-found booth to your children wherever you go.)

Here's an example of how to use your outings as a learning laboratory: When you're in a store, ask your child to point out who he would go to for help if he got separated from you. Then take him over to the security guard and ask that person, "What would you do if my child came and asked you for help? What would he need to tell you?" These real-life interviews leave lasting impressions on your kids and make the idea of approaching someone for help much easier for them.

Staying with You in a Crowd or Public Place

You must teach children not to wander off in a crowd or a public place. With very young children, I recommend that you keep them within arm's length at all times. With preschoolers and young grade-school children who tend to walk behind or run ahead, show them *exactly* how close they must stay to you. Say, "This is close to Daddy. This is not." And then, enforce it. It is crucial that you be able to see them at all times—in stores, at parks, in a crowd. The rule of thumb is, the more people around, the closer your child should be to you.

Say to your small child before an outing, "One of our rules is that you do not run away from Mommy or Daddy," and then, when you get to your destination, ask, "What's one of our most important rules?" Praise your child when he repeats the rule back to you. Offer children who are extremely active a small reward for remembering to stay close to you at all times.

THE REPORTING RULE

From the time your child is a toddler, encourage her to report in. Before she heads down the hall or into the backyard, tell her to check in with you. This will teach her to give you ongoing bulletins about her whereabouts. When you take your preschooler to the park, say, "Tell me when you're done at the swings and want to go play on the monkey bars." At day care or preschool, your child must also use the reporting rule by telling the adult in charge before she leaves to use the bathroom.

As your children enter grade school, you may permit them to go next door or a few doors down to a friend's house. Again, reinforce the idea that they must always ask you for permission before they leave. And, even more importantly, they must *never* change plans or directions between their house and their destination, not until they have checked back with you. If you can't be sure your child would obey such a rule—or if you don't live in a safe neighborhood—use an alternative system.

Here's a way to allow your child a little independence in his neighborhood that works for many families. Before your child leaves for a friend's house, alert the friend's parent that your child is on the way and ask her to watch out for him. Then, see your child off and continue watching him from the sidewalk or yard until he gets to his friend's safely.

To teach a child how to avoid being intercepted on her walk to a friend's, I recommend role-playing or a puppet show. Pretend with your child that she is walking to a friend's house after getting your permission. Then play a variety of characters who try to intercept her between home and her destination. One time you might pretend to be another child who invites your daughter to come to her house instead of her friend's. Another time you're a friendly neighbor who invites her in for a glass of lemonade. And then, play a man who offers her a kitten or some other enticing gift from the back of his van.

Grade-schoolers who spend more time on their own or with friends are more susceptible to people who might try to persuade them to make an exception to the reporting rule, according to Penelope Leach. A man with lines like "I'm sure your mom would say it's OK" or "Let's not bother Mommy; we'll be back in a minute" may be successful in tricking a child to go with him. Grade-schoolers must also be prepared for any adult in uniform who approaches them and says, "There's a problem. You must come with me."

"What if . . .?" scenarios and role-playing are very effective in preparing your child to avoid these common tricks. During your discussions, reinforce the idea that no one who cares about you would ask you to make an exception to the reporting rule.

As your children get older, you will revise the reporting rule. You may allow your preteens to come and go more freely within agreeable limits. If they have been willing to check in with you up until now, they are more likely to agree to sensible limits and follow certain precautions. See chapter 11 for specific strategies to use when your children want—and can handle—more freedom.

WHEN A STRANGER ASKS FOR HELP

You can use a variety of learning activities to strengthen your children's ability to refuse requests for help from strangers. Some of the suggestions below come from parents who have taught this skill.

Role-play several scenarios with younger children. Tell your child that you are the stranger who is going to ask for help. Tell him he is the child who must decide whether or not to help the stranger. Then, play your role to the hilt: try to evoke sympathy and be as appealing as possible. (You can also ask an adult friend to play the role of the stranger, while you supervise.)

Here are some suggested scenes to enact:

- A stranger who asks the child to come over to the car and give him directions. (The child stands ten to twenty feet back from the car and tells the man to go to a gas station for help.)
- A stranger who asks for help looking for one of his contact lenses that fell on the sidewalk. (The child says, "I'm sorry I can't help you" and quickly walks away, making sure she isn't followed.)
- A stranger who acts distressed about her lost pet and tries to enlist the child's help to search for it. (The child says, "I'm sorry I can't help you" and quickly walks away, making sure he isn't followed.)

Each time your child refuses to help the stranger, praise him for his "good judgment" or "safe decision." If your child errs and goes to the stranger, stop and discuss why this behavior is dangerous. Then practice the scene again.

If you don't want to role-play these scenes, you could use "What if . . . ?" questions, particularly with older children. However, given how effective this request for help ploy is, I'd encourage you to continually reinforce the message they must not help a stranger who asks for assistance.

Also, take the time to demonstrate what "three giant steps" back from the street look like. Drive your car up to the curb and have your child practice taking three giant steps back. Have him do this when you pull up to the curb or slowly drive along beside him. Ask your child why he thinks taking three steps back is a good idea. Then the next time you're walking in the neighborhood, ask your child to show you again what three giant steps from the curb look like.

Younger children, in addition to enjoying playing these scenes with you, may want to reverse roles. They love being the person who is trying to trick you. By the way, be sure to miss an answer or two so that they can explain what you did wrong and why. During your practice, reinforce the idea that children have the right to say no to any adult asking for help, and that if someone asks them for assistance, they should be prepared to quickly run away in the opposite direction.

"YELL, RUN, AND TELL"

Nicole: Get away from me! Leave me alone! I don't know you!

Mother: That was great. And I liked how you used your biggest, strongest voice. Then, what do you do next?

Nicole: Run away, and go tell an adult.

Mother: That's right. . . . Well, from what I've seen, you'd be able to use "Yell, Run, and Tell" with no problem.

"Yell, Run, and Tell" is easy for kids to remember, and it gives them three steps to follow in case of an attempted abduction. Prepare your child with the specific words to say if someone grabs him in public. "No! No! You're not my father! He's kidnapping me!" is a good way to deter an abductor and attract help. It's likely to be more effective than "Help!" or "Stop!" because passersby often misinterpret these scenes as family arguments. When they see an adult struggling with a young child, sometimes they conclude that the child is having a tantrum. In several well-publicized tragedies, that's what the abductors told concerned citizens who stepped in to help.

The words that your child uses to enlist help should immediately signal to people:

- This person is not known to him.
- He is being taken against his will.
- He needs help.

Every child should be prepared with simple lines they can yell in an emergency. But what if your child seems reluctant or shy about drawing attention to herself? She says she would feel "too embarrassed" to create a scene. Then you must help her develop her willingness to openly resist an abductor. Tell her directly that being compliant or passive puts her in more danger. Then take her to some deserted place and have her practice shouting at the top of her lungs. Reassure quiet children that creating a scene in an emergency is a courageous thing to do. Emphasize to them that making a big scene is critical to their safety.

ESTABLISHING AND FOLLOWING A SAFE ROUTE

Here are two different parents with two very different children. Here's how they established a safety route with their kids:

Parent #1: My son won't sit still long enough to draw a map. But he was happy to lead me on the safety route and point out the places he'd be careful. It was fun for both of us because along the way I tried all sorts of ways to get him off the safety route. I tempted him with money, baseball tickets, and even called him a "wimp" when he wouldn't take a shortcut. We laughed a lot and got in some good practice.

Parent #2: My daughter seemed unwilling to walk with her friends this past fall. I think she'd heard too many stories about kids being kidnapped. Anyway, what seemed to work is that for a while we practiced walking to and from school on the weekends. We talked about points along the way where she should stay alert. I pointed out where people lived who were often home when she was walking to and from school, people who she could ask for help. And I reminded her about safety tips she already knew, like how far to stay back from the curb. She would never dream of taking a shortcut, so most of my job was to reassure her that she could walk to school safely. Well, after a few weekends of this and three weeks of driving her every day, she told me she wanted to walk to school with her friends.

STAYING WITH A FRIEND AT ALL TIMES

Because children who are alone make easy targets, it's good to have a safety rule about staying with others. You don't want to alarm your child with horrible tales of children being snatched off the streets, so your approach should be positive and matter-of-fact: "It's important that you and Hannah walk together and that you not take shortcuts. In case I ever need to find you, I want to be sure who you're with and where I can look for you."

If your child tends to be a loner or gets distracted while with others, you need to emphasize your child's responsibilities in being on the streets without adult supervision. Also, spend additional practice on developing your child's awareness and observation skills.

OBSERVING AND RECALLING IMPORTANT DETAILS

Teach children to look for and recall specific details. Your child will regain some sense of control after an incident by aiding law enforcement officers in apprehending the criminal.

- Organize details: Start with the person's head and work your way down, noting the attacker's sex, race, approximate age, height, build, hair type, and complexion.
- Note the time and place of the incident.
- Note particular words and phrases used by the attacker.
- Note unusual characteristics like birthmarks, missing teeth, or scars.
- Note the license plate number, color, and make of the attacker's car.
- Write down as many details as possible after the incident, while they are fresh in your child's mind, even before the police arrive.

A good learning activity to promote memory skills is to ask your children to note as many details as they can in a thirty-second period—about a person, a street, or a car. When the time is up, have them close their eyes and recall as much information as possible while you write it down. Coach your children to give you the information in categories, as shown above, which will help them recall more details. Then compare your notes with what they observed and remembered. Another learning activity is to memorize license plates when you're driving around town. Have your child select a car and memorize its license plate number while you write it down. Then ask your child to tell you the number two or three minutes later.

ANSWERING THE PHONE AND DOOR SAFELY

Practice safe telephone behavior. Give your child scripts to use in answering the phone (see chapter 8). Then, using play telephones, listen to how well your child sticks to the script as you ask different questions. If your son or daughter is too open or talkative, even with practice, postpone phone-answering privileges for a while.

Earlier in this chapter, I suggested enacting "The Three Little Pigs" at the front door to assess how easily your young child can be enticed into opening it. If you discover that your child is easy prey to the ploys used by adults who try to gain access to your home, simply withhold the privilege until you feel your child can show some restraint and judgment in how he behaves toward strangers at the front door.

Remember, because it isn't essential that your young child answer either the door or the phone, you can give her more time to develop the maturity to handle these responsibilities. In the meantime, model good behavior and give her opportunities to practice how to answer the phone and door safely.

STAYING AWAY FROM CARS

Since most stranger abductions involve enticing or forcing children into cars, let's give some extra attention to how you can help your children avoid them. Below are two learning activities that will strengthen your child's resistance to abductors' ploys.

With a younger child, act out stories using puppets and cars and ask her to decide if it's OK for her "child" puppet to get in the car with the "adult" puppet.

1.   Have the adult puppet try to bribe the child puppet into coming over to his car. Tempt the child puppet with wonderful

things you know your daughter likes. Be friendly, interested, and playful. If the child puppet comes over to the car, don't correct her. Instead, gently stop the show and ask your daughter, "What is your puppet thinking right now?" Most likely, your daughter's answer will reveal a lack of information or faulty logic.

Suggest that you switch roles and act out the story again. This time let your child try to entice you. This gives you the opportunity to model the appropriate response. You might step back from the curb and say, "Go away! I don't know you!" and run for help. Afterward, if your child is willing, switch roles again and let her be the safety-conscious puppet. When she demonstrates the correct response, praise her for remembering the rule about not accepting treats, gifts, or invitations from strangers.

2.   Using role-playing or a puppet show, try to persuade your daughter to ignore the authorized driver rule. Attempt to trick her by saying there's been an accident—or there's an emergency—and that you've been asked to pick her up. If she asks for the code word, tell her that in all the commotion, her parents forgot to tell it to you. Then, depending on your child's response—she should *not* go with you—either praise her or repeat the steps outlined in the first example.

There's no better way to increase children's defense against abductors and molesters in cars than to practice these possible scenarios. Older children, while beyond the stage of enjoying puppet shows, can engage in safety conversations with you. Discuss different scenarios with them, such as the one where the stranger asks the child to come over to the car to help him read his map. Encourage them to be good problem solvers and critical thinkers. Listen for mistakes in judgment. What leads them to make unsafe decisions? When does their logic fail? Wherever your children show signs of weakness or confusion intensify your teaching efforts, and continue to supervise them until they have demonstrated their ability to consistently make wise choices.

Developing Your Own Learning Activity

In this section, I'll walk you through the process of developing a learning activity. At the end, you'll have a custom-designed learning activity to use with your child. (You may want to do this for each of your children, so I suggest you write out your answers on a separate piece of paper.) By doing some preparation now, you'll be more able to take advantage of spontaneous "teachable moments" later.

1. Select one personal safety skill to teach.
   The personal safety skill I want to teach is _____
   _____
   _____.

2. Write down 3 things that you and your child enjoy doing together.
   a. _____
   b. _____
   c. _____

3. What activities does your child enjoy? Check all answers that apply. There is extra space to write in other activities.

   ___painting/drawing/
      coloring   ___puzzles   ___dancing
   ___music   ___swimming   ___hiking
   ___fantasy/pretend   ___gymnastics   ___reading
   ___watching or   ___riding bicycles ___watching TV
      playing sports   ___building/fixing
   ___playing board   things
      games
   ___playing computer
      games   ___other_____

4. What errands and routines do you and your child do together?

a. _____

b. _____

c. _____

Your answers in questions 2, 3, and 4 provide useful information. From those answers, you can plan learning activities around your joint interests (#2), around your child's interests (#3), or around a simple routine that you do together (#4).

5. Choose an activity based on your answers to questions 2, 3, or 4 and write it in the first blank below. Write down the personal-safety skill you chose in the second blank. Additional suggestions are provided in the box.

My plan is to use this activity, _____

_____

_____

_____

to teach this personal-safety skill, _____

_____

_____

_____.

6. As you plan your learning activity, think about these things:
   a. Can you get the information across in 15 minutes or less?
   b. What materials will you need?
   c. Is the activity practical and simple?

7. In the space below, develop your learning activity. Write down specifically what you'll do and say to teach the safety information.

_____

_____

_____

_____

_____

_____

You don't have to write out your learning activities each time, but you do need to think about them in advance. As you experiment with what works best with your child, you'll feel more confident and will need less preparation time.

Suggested Methods

- Make up or rewrite familiar stories together with your child as the main—and safety-conscious—character.
- Draw/paint pictures that illustrate an important message.
- Play "What if . . . " games. (What would you do if you were at the park and . . . ?)
- Role-play to act out safety situations.
- Make up and perform puppet or doll "shows" that teach safety rules.
- Make up a rhyme or song to foster memorization.
- Use outings in your community as your teaching laboratory.
- Use videotapes, cassettes, and books to introduce safety information.
- Make posters "advertising" an important safety message.
- Have your child draw safe route maps.
- Draw pictures contrasting safe and unsafe behavior (and their consequences).

Teaching Personal Safety Over Time

Because you teach personal safety as a series of steps over time, it's important to monitor your children's progress and to keep your goals in mind. The following system is designed to help you track what you teach, and to set some time lines for teaching it.

Your Preschooler's Personal-Safety Skills

1. Can he name all parts of the body?
   a. Yes_____ No_____
   b. If you have not begun to teach this skill, set a target date to begin teaching it: I will start teaching this skill_____, 19_____.
   c. Skill mastered_____, 19_____.

2. Can she identify which parts of the body are private?
   a. Yes_____ No_____
   b. If you have not begun to teach this skill, set a target date to begin teaching it: I will start teaching this skill_____, 19_____.
   c. Skill mastered_____, 19_____.

3. Does he know what "OK" and "Not OK" touches are?
   a. Yes_____ No_____
   b. If you have not begun to teach this skill, set a target date to begin teaching it: I will start teaching this skill_____, 19_____.
   c. Skill mastered_____, 19_____.

4. Does she know who to approach for help?
   a. Yes_____ No_____
   b. If you have not begun to teach this skill, set a target date to begin teaching it: I will start teaching this skill_____, 19_____.
   c. Skill mastered_____, 19_____.

5. Does he know his address and phone number?
   a. Yes_____ No_____

    b. If you have not begun to teach this skill, set a target date
       to begin teaching it: I will start teaching this
       skill_____, 19_____.

    c. Skill mastered_____, 19_____.

6. Can she recall her address and phone number under
   stress?
    a. Yes____ No____
    b. If you have not begun to teach this skill, set a target date
       to begin teaching it: I will start teaching this
       skill_____, 19_____.
    c. Skill mastered_____, 19_____.

7. Does he know when and how to phone 0 and 911?
    a. Yes____ No____
    b. If you have not begun to teach this skill, set a target date
       to begin teaching it: I will start teaching this
       skill_____, 19_____.
    c. Skill mastered_____, 19_____.

8. Does she know what a stranger is?
    a. Yes____ No____
    b. If you have not begun to teach this skill, set a target date
       to begin teaching it: I will start teaching this
       skill_____, 19_____.
    c. Skill mastered_____, 19_____.

YOUR GRADE-SCHOOLER'S PERSONAL-SAFETY SKILLS

1. Can she interact safely with strangers?
    a. Yes____ No____
    b. If you have not begun to teach this skill, set a
       target date to begin teaching it: I will start teaching
       this skill_____, 19_____.
    c. Skill mastered_____, 19_____.

2. Can he refuse invitations and gifts from strangers?
   a. Yes_____ No_____
   b. If you have not begun to teach this skill, set a target date to begin teaching it: I will start teaching this skill_____, 19_____.
   c. Skill mastered_____, 19_____.

3. Can she answer the telephone without revealing too much information?
   a. Yes_____ No_____
   b. If you have not begun to teach this skill, set a target date to begin teaching it: I will start teaching this skill_____, 19_____.
   c. Skill mastered_____, 19_____.

4. Does he know how to respond to a stranger at the door?
   a. Yes_____ No_____
   b. If you have not begun to teach this skill, set a target date to begin teaching it: I will start teaching this skill_____, 19_____.
   c. Skill mastered_____, 19_____.

5. Can she "Yell, Run, and Tell"?
   a. Yes_____ No_____
   b. If you have not begun to teach this skill, set a target date to begin teaching it: I will start teaching this skill_____, 19_____.
   c. Skill mastered_____, 19_____.

6. Can he turn down rides from people who don't know the family code word?
   a. Yes_____ No_____
   b. If you have not begun to teach this skill, set a target date to begin teaching it: I will start teaching this skill_____, 19_____.
   c. Skill mastered_____, 19_____.

7. Can she follow the reporting rule consistently?
   a. Yes_____ No_____
   b. If you have not begun to teach this skill, set a target date to begin teaching it: I will start teaching this skill_____, 19_____.
   c. Skill mastered_____, 19_____.

8. Does he know what to do if separated from you?
   a. Yes_____ No_____
   b. If you have not begun to teach this skill, set a target date to begin teaching it: I will start teaching this skill_____, 19_____.
   c. Skill mastered_____, 19_____.

9. Can she recognize uncomfortable feelings?
   a. Yes_____ No_____
   b. If you have not begun to teach this skill, set a target date to begin teaching it: I will start teaching this skill_____, 19_____.
   c. Skill mastered_____, 19_____.

10. Can he comply with family safety rules, including the "stay with a buddy at all times" rule?
    a. Yes_____ No_____
    b. If you have not begun to teach this skill, set a target date to begin teaching it: I will start teaching this skill_____, 19_____.
    c. Skill mastered_____, 19_____.

11. Can she refuse a dare under pressure?
    a. Yes_____ No_____
    b. If you have not begun to teach this skill, set a target date to begin teaching it: I will start teaching this skill_____, 19_____.
    c. Skill mastered_____, 19_____.

12. Can he discuss sensitive or confusing feelings with you?
    a. Yes_____ No_____
    b. If you have not begun to teach this skill, set a target date
       to begin teaching it: I will start teaching this
       skill_____, 19_____.
    c. Skill mastered_____, 19_____.

13. Can she say no to unwanted touches, even those initiated
    during games?
    a. Yes_____ No_____
    b. If you have not begun to teach this skill, set a target date
       to begin teaching it: I will start teaching this
       skill_____, 19_____.
    c. Skill mastered_____, 19_____.

14. Can he question and report any confusing or inappropriate
    behavior from baby-sitters, relatives, friends, etc.?
    a. Yes_____ No_____
    b. If you have not begun to teach this skill, set a target date
       to begin teaching it: I will start teaching this
       skill_____, 19_____.
    c. Skill mastered_____, 19_____.

15. Does she know how to identify a real law enforcement offi-
    cer and understand that not all people wearing a badge or
    uniform are safe?
    a. Yes_____ No_____
    b. If you have not begun to teach this skill, set a target date
       to begin teaching it: I will start teaching this
       skill_____, 19_____.
    c. Skill mastered_____, 19_____.

16. Can he report any adult who threatens him not to share a
    secret with anyone?
    a. Yes_____ No_____
    b. If you have not begun to teach this skill, set a target date

to begin teaching it: I will start teaching this
skill_____, 19_____.
c. Skill mastered_____, 19_____.

Key Points

- Remember the five steps to your child's personal safety: Protect, Prepare, Practice, Prompt, and Preview.
- Preschoolers and grade-school children learn differently. Adjust your teaching approach as your child gets older.
- Use what you know about your child—his interests, the way he likes to learn, what his strengths are—to plan enjoyable learning activities.
- Keep learning activities simple, practical, and no more than fifteen minutes long. They should be designed to fit into your life.
- Each learning session should end on a positive note with your child having an improved sense of accomplishment or mastery.
- Look for and use teachable moments in your everyday life so that personal safety fits naturally into your activities and routines.
- Make sure in communicating safety concepts that you use words and phrases that are easy to understand. Maintain a positive and matter-of-fact approach during your learning activities and safety discussions.
- Evaluate how well your children have learned new safety information by providing them with supervised opportunities to demonstrate their understanding and skill. Review these skills regularly.

CHAPTER 11

When They Want More Freedom

As your children enter the upper elementary grades, their world expands to include more activities, more people, and, usually, more freedom. Some kids who have been in after-school programs since kindergarten now want to "hang out" rather than be in structured activities all day. Many are in charge of themselves after school. And others get so involved in clubs and youth groups that they are likely to see more of their peers than their families. How much freedom you grant your children is up to you to decide. But most kids get their first taste of freedom in their preteen years. How they can manage it safely is the focus of this chapter.

In chapter 10, I told you that teaching safety over time is a process of five steps: protecting, preparing, practicing, prompting, and previewing. I showed you how to lay the foundation for basic personal-safety skills when your children are in preschool (protect) and then how to help your children develop and practice safety skills when they are between the ages of six and nine (prepare and practice). Now, as your children approach adolescence, your primary job is to prompt and preview.

Prompting and Previewing

Prompting children means regularly reminding them to use the safety skills they have learned. Prompting also means providing them with opportunities to use what they have learned. When you anticipate what skills your children will need to handle a new situation and then you talk about or teach them those skills beforehand, it's called previewing. Whenever your children are facing a new responsibility or challenge, it's essential to identify and discuss the relevant safety information that will help them handle it well.

Let's say you are a single parent taking your children to an amusement park. Your seven-year-old daughter brings a friend along and so does your eleven-year-old son. Because your kids have very different interests, staying together at all times won't be practical. On the way to the park, your son and his friend ask if they can go on the rides by themselves. How do you make your decision? Do you say yes because it solves the problem of trying to be in two places at once?

When I pose this question to parents in my workshops, the first answer I usually get is, "It depends on how responsible the boy and his friend are." That's a pretty good place to start. But I encourage parents to get more specific. In addition to how well the boys have handled responsibility before, the parent should also evaluate how well prepared they are to handle the *specific* kinds of problems they might encounter while in an amusement park. It's a good idea to shift the focus from how responsible the boys usually are to evaluating what *demonstrable skills* they have for managing themselves at the park.

This is where prompting and previewing safety information come in. The parent can discuss several "What if . . . ?" scenarios with the boys.

What would you do if a group of kids started to bother you?
What would you do if you got separated from each other?
What would you do if one of you got hurt?

If she is satisfied with their responses, the next thing to do is to give them some general rules for the day like "If we're not at the Ferris wheel at three o'clock, wait ten minutes and then head to the Information booth."

In general, taking children into a crowded public place requires some reviewing of safety procedures. To the seven-year-olds, the mother might say: "The boardwalk will be crowded today. Stick together and hold hands when there are a lot of people around. Remember, I need to be able to see you at all times. Also, if we get separated, let's agree to meet at the merry-go-round."

In the next example, a twelve-year-old girl asks her father to let her go downtown with her friends.

Jessica: I want to take the bus downtown with my friends on Friday after school. We want to do some shopping. May I go?

Father: Well, first let's take a minute to talk about how you would handle taking the bus and being downtown on your own.

Jessica: But we've gone over that before! I know what to do!

Father: I realize we've discussed this, but it's been a while and I want to review a few important things with you.

Notice that this parent didn't win any popularity contests for insisting that his daughter discuss how she will handle herself on this shopping trip. Some parents avoid these conversations because older children tend to complain about them. One father I know didn't like his twelve-year-old daughter's protests, so he decided not to "push it." Recently, he discovered she had been lying to him about her whereabouts and the amount of time she was spending with a boyfriend.

As your children get older, expect that your reminders to be careful will be met with "I know that! You don't have to tell me!" or "You worry too much. I can take care of myself." Ignore your children's protests. Let them know you care and don't let your kids' resistance override your need for peace of mind. Do what the father in the last example did. Gently, but firmly, insist that they discuss how they will handle a privilege so that you can decide if you will grant it.

What are three possible "What if . . . ?" questions this father should ask? (Here's a clue: They should relate to public transportation, peer pressure, and being downtown.)

1. What would you do if the bus was late?
2. What would you do if your friends wanted to do something wrong, like shoplifting?
3. What would you do if a stranger approached you on the street?

What responses to the above questions would demonstrate the daughter's ability to handle potential problems while downtown with her friends?

1. I would call you if I was going to be late getting home or if we needed a ride.
2. If my friends did something wrong, I'd tell them to cut it out and I wouldn't do it.
3. If a stranger approached me, I'd get ready to Yell, Run, and Tell.

Before making his final decision, this parent should also consider how safe the areas are in which she will be traveling and shopping and how well she has handled previous outings with these friends.

As a parent, it is your right and responsibility to ask your child to prove that she can handle a given situation, especially one that will be unsupervised. Your role is to anticipate several problems she might encounter in that specific situation and ask "What if . . . ?" questions that will reveal how safely she would respond. Here are two more situations where you would want proof that your child can use good judgment before you say yes.

Before you allow your daughter and a friend to go to a

movie theater several miles away, you might say, "So, you get out of the movie and Jenny's mother doesn't show up to give you a ride home. You call Jenny's mom and no one answers. Tell me what you would do next." (The girls should call you for a ride and not attempt to get home on their own.)

Before you allow your child to go to the convenience store—a favorite spot for abductors and molesters—you might say, "You are at the store and a man comes over and starts talking to you. What would you do if ignoring him didn't make him go away?" (The child should tell the cashier about the problem and decide whether or not to call the police. Then he should wait at the checkout counter until the man leaves or the police arrive. He also needs to decide whether it's safe to walk home. If he is unsure, he should call you for a ride.)

On the other hand, you don't want to seem intrusive with your questioning. Once your child has demonstrated good judgment in one situation, there is no need to start over with similar questions the next time. At that point, you want to reinforce responsible behavior and encourage positive independence with comments like "The last time I let you go into town for ice cream you handled it very well. As long as you can remember what we talked about, I'm happy to let you go again."

Sometimes, in order to make a decision, you'll need to do both—prompt *and* preview safety information. For example, let's say your ten-year-old son wants to walk to school with his friends. Consider that the boy has the following safety skills:

- He knows his address and phone number.
- He knows how to reach you by phone at your work number.
- He crosses the street safely.
- He follows traffic signals.
- He knows the safe route to and from school.
- He stays with friends or an adult most of the time (although he sometimes runs ahead or lags behind).
- With help, he observes who and what is around him.

- He identifies helping people in his neighborhood, but is hesitant to ask anyone for help.
- He understands that he may accept rides only from authorized drivers, but has forgotten the code word in the past.

Based on this boy's current safety skills, there are four skills on this list that he should successfully demonstrate before you allow him to walk to school unsupervised. They are:

1. To stay with his friends at all times—he is not consistent about this.
2. To be alert to potential dangers in his environment—so far he can do this with help from an adult but not on his own.
3. To ask for help in an emergency—he is reluctant to approach people.
4. To remember the code word for drivers authorized to pick him up in a car—he has forgotten it in the past.

Let's take one of the skills for which your son needs prompting: being alert to potential dangers in his environment. To reinforce this skill, try going for a walk together along the designated route. During the walk, ask him to point out any danger spots: a bad crossing or a deserted building. To help him build his skill and self-confidence, ask him to tell you what to stay alert for and what to avoid. Praise him when he demonstrates good observation skills. Repeat this exercise until you have proof that he can stay alert and aware of his surroundings. For the other three areas in which he needs more practice, design simple learning activities to strengthen those particular skills (see chapter 10 for ideas). Then grant him the privilege of walking with his friends as soon as you *both* agree he's fully prepared to handle it.

Whenever your children are facing new responsibilities and challenges, you need to take the time to prepare them. It's important to update personal-safety information to fit the new situation, to review or practice the skills that may be needed, and to repeat the skill practice until your children consistently demonstrate their ability to act safely.

Don't be surprised if, at this stage, your kids are less interested in learning activities and safety discussions. And don't even attempt to lecture, because they will tune you out in a second. In most cases, brief conversations are sufficient, unless you're just beginning to teach a safety skill. (As we discussed, you must teach a new skill a little bit at a time and over time.) A brief safety-review discussion may take less than a minute. By thinking about the following points ahead of time, you'll ensure that you get the information you need if you:

- Know what safety information you want to reinforce.
- Make your remarks brief.
- Check for understanding.
- Make sure your children agree to what you expect from them.

For example, if you have a rule about checking in, and your daughter sometimes likes to stay after her youth meeting to visit with her friends, you might say the following: "I don't mind you staying a while after your meeting, but if you stay more than fifteen minutes, you need to call. Do we have a deal?"

If she resists the idea of letting you know of any changes in her plans, you might say: "Each person in our family has the responsibility of calling home if their plans change. It's both a courtesy and our family safety policy. Can I count on you to call if you're going to be more than fifteen minutes late getting home?"

Notice that before you end the conversation you must get her agreement to call if she will be delayed or wants to change her plans. If you've been establishing family safety policies from the beginning, your preteens will be more likely to agree to sensible limits and precautions now.

For preteens, prompting and previewing safety information:

- helps them anticipate possible dangers they may encounter
- reassures them by giving them a sense of control over a new or unknown situation
- equips them to handle any problems that might arise in a given situation by having updated and specific safety information

For parents, prompting and previewing safety information:

- signals which skills need review or practice
- helps them determine how much supervision their kids need, if any
- reinforces their kids' commitment to act responsibly

Remember, as your children approach adolescence, it's natural for them to seek more independence. The best you can do is to prepare them for it now, because they'll insist on having more freedom soon.

Making Your Neighborhood Safe

Crime is not inevitable, and we as individuals can make our neighborhoods safer for our children—and for all of us—by getting involved with our neighbors and organizing a Neighborhood Watch group. One of the benefits is that Neighborhood Watch programs usually establish a "safe house" on each block, a home run by a qualified adult that children are taught to recognize and go to if they need help. Safe houses can serve as a refuge from gangs or bullies as well as a place to get help if there is an accident.

Another benefit of establishing a Neighborhood Watch program is that it builds a sense of solidarity among neighbors. This is particularly important in neighborhoods plagued by crime. The neighborhood I live in has a Neighborhood Alert program. The process for starting your own group is simple. Here are some tips, courtesy of Westec Security, Inc.

- Contact your local police department and talk to their crime prevention officer about organizing a Neighborhood Watch group. This officer will help you get organized and attend your first meeting.
- Talk to your neighbors and tell them that you are starting a Neighborhood Watch group and that you need their participation.
- Enlist the help of another neighbor. Introduce yourselves by going door-to-door.
- Ask your neighbors which evenings and times during the week are the best for them to meet. Generally, neighborhood meetings are conducted at 7:00 or 7:30 P.M., Mondays through Thursdays.
- Also discuss the most convenient and available place to hold the meetings. Ask your neighbors if they would like to offer their homes as a meeting site. Other meeting locations may be a centrally located church, synagogue, school, or meeting hall.
- Exchange phone numbers. Tell your neighbors that you will notify them when a meeting is scheduled.
- Take this opportunity to become acquainted on a first-name basis. This is important for a successful Neighborhood Watch program.
- Contact your crime prevention officer to schedule the time and date of your first meeting. He or she will help you get the word out and encourage people to attend.
- Remind everyone a few days before the meeting, either by phone or in person, to insure a good turnout.
- Become familiar with your neighbors' routines.
- Keep a trusted neighbor informed if your house will be unoccupied for an extended period of time.

- Look after your neighbors' homes when they are away and ask them to look after yours.
- Post Neighborhood Watch signs on your street and in windows. Advertise the fact that yours is a Neighborhood Watch community.

Self-Defense Products

There is a growing trend today to promote everything from self-defense classes to personal-safety alarms. In some ways, I see this as a positive sign, an indicator that society is recognizing the need to address the issue of child safety. In other ways, I think this is a sign that *fear sells*.

An article in the *Los Angeles Times* on January 9, 1994, summed up the worst of what is happening now. The writer began by saying: "First came crime. Then came fear. And then came the sales pitch." Parents must be aware that high-priced products and classes alone are not adequate. There is no substitute for teaching personal-safety skills to your children. And there is no device or self-defense class that will practice those skills with your kids and supervise them until they can use what they have learned.

When there's a crime in your area, it's perfectly natural to feel alarmed or fearful. At that point, you may be willing to do or buy anything for some peace of mind. Be aware that some promoters prey on the fears of parents. You need to evaluate personal-safety products and services. Don't panic, reach for a quick-fix solution, or turn your responsibility to protect your children over to someone else.

A product named PAAL is a palm-size electronic alarm that emits a shrieking noise when activated. Parents must remember that devices work only if children have the time and presence of mind to activate them. In one recent publicized kidnapping in the Midwest, a girl was abducted off the street and killed. Her beeper was found on the ground near the curb.

Keep in mind that unless your child's *inner* alarm goes off in time, no device will do him much good. A personal alarm can't tell a child what his sixth sense can—it can't warn him *before* he's in danger. Once again, it's up to parents to teach children how to identify, trust, and act on their gut feelings. If a child hasn't learned how to do that, carrying a personal-safety device may be useless.

Alarms require one hand to activate them and cost between thirty and forty dollars. Whistles, which require the same amount of agility, cost about a dollar. On the other hand, yelling doesn't cost anything and effectively deters most abductors. Shouts of "Help! This man's trying to kidnap me!" or "Leave me alone! I don't know you!" will thwart most kidnappers. What you get when you buy a personal alarm is a very loud sound and the promise that this sound will scare away any assailant. It's good to remember that while a high, piercing noise can be heard farther away than a human voice, it's a nonspecific noise. In other words, at night, or even during the day, someone might hear the alarm and think, "Oh, it's just another car alarm going off," and tune it out.

Besides the false sense of security we may get from providing our children with personal-safety alarms, it's also very tempting to think that a class in self-defense will protect them.

Home Alone and in Charge

We live in an era where movies about kids having to fend for themselves become box-office hits. In the film *Home Alone* and its sequel, *Home Alone II*, a ten-year-old boy single-handedly foils two burglars who try to break in while his family is on vacation. He is home alone because his family accidentally leaves him behind.

The premise of two parents loaded down with kids and luggage forgetting a child in their rush to the airport seems highly unlikely, but not totally impossible. The boy's mental and mechanical genius for outsmarting the burglars is sheer fantasy, however—and kids love it.

This story holds definite appeal for children who worry about being alone or about being forgotten by busy parents. Its real impact comes at the end, when the boy triumphs over being home alone and becomes a hero in the eyes of the police and his family. As the credits roll, the boy, who was often harassed by his stepbrothers and -sisters and misunderstood by his parents, beams a smile that says he is now loved and appreciated. This movie offers reassuring fantasies to every child who has been left home alone or who has ever felt forgotten.

In the United States, there are 22.4 million women in the workforce with children under age eighteen. Statistics show that most children age ten and older are on their own after school. That means that on any given school day, 15 million children are in charge of themselves for an hour or more.

The term "latchkey kid" has been replaced by less pejorative phrases like "kids in charge" or "kids responsible for their self-care." But the main reasons kids stay home alone haven't changed. Children aren't being supervised after school primarily because parents can't afford child care or after-school programs or because they don't have relatives nearby who can help. The parents I meet whose kids are home alone tell me that they would prefer to leave their school-age children in child-care centers or with relatives or baby-sitters. But such accommodations are not always available or may be financially out of the question.

In this section, I will not discuss the need for our government and our workplaces to provide better and more affordable child care. Instead, I'll focus on two things: first, how to assess whether or not children are ready to be in charge of themselves after school, and second, how to turn being home alone into a positive and constructive arrangement.

There are several things to consider in making the choice to leave a child home alone. Age is only one consideration. You must also take into account the child's maturity, personality, and level of independent skill. The box on page 194 lists things to observe and ask before you decide to leave your child home alone.

Observe:
- Can your child usually be relied on to obey rules?
- Is your child afraid of the dark?
- Does your child seem to be extremely afraid of unexplained noises?
- Do your children get along well enough to stay home together?
- How does your child react to being left with a sitter or a relative?
- Can your child solve problems?
- Can your child make emergency phone calls and give the necessary information?
- Can your child lock and unlock the door?

Ask:
- Do you want to take care of yourself?
- What are your feelings and thoughts about being alone?
- Would you prefer to be alone, with a sitter, or in an after-school program?
- Can you and your brothers and sisters get along?
- Do you feel nervous if a stranger telephones or knocks on the door?
- What do you do when you hear strange noises anywhere in the house?

Questions are adapted from *Latchkey Kids: Their Safety and Care*, The Family Forum Library, © 1992, The Bureau for At-Risk Youth, Huntington, NY 11743, 1-800-99-YOUTH.

According to authors Marilyn Dreilinger, M.A., and Ron Kerner, Ph.D., what you observe will help you determine how ready your child is for the responsibilities that come with self-care. They caution that pushing these responsibilities on kids can create the kind of fear that undermines self-confidence and interferes with success in school or other activities.

Dreilinger and Kerner suggest that by observing your children's behavior and asking questions, you will get clues about their fears and anxieties that must be taken seriously. For example, one child may enjoy the solitude of self-care and happily entertain herself or do homework. Another child may not be ready to be left alone. He is fearful of noises, worried something will happen; he stays inside and frets until someone comes home. The same applies to a child who puts on all the lights, turns the sound on the television up to full volume, and suffers from nightmares.

There are other considerations as well. How safe is your neighborhood? Is it safe for children to be left unattended where you live? Who is usually around your neighborhood in the afternoon?

In thinking about how your children get along with each other, consider how often they are able to settle disputes on their own and how often they need an adult to intervene. If sibling arguments in your family routinely escalate into physical fights, you will need to make separate arrangements for your children after school.

Another consideration is how close by you are. Are you accessible by phone and can you get home quickly in an emergency? In the San Francisco area, parents often live in one community and work in another. Some parents consciously choose not to work across the Bay from where they live, because major bridges are often blocked or closed to traffic when there is an accident or a chemical spill. In setting up your child-care and work arrangements, it's important to consider how you will stay in touch with your kids at all times, as well as what you will do in an emergency. Consider in advance how you and your children will manage if you are delayed by a late meeting, a traffic jam, or a natural disaster.

IF THEY WANT TO STAY HOME ALONE

If, after observing your children and asking them questions, you come to the conclusions that (1) they are unafraid of staying alone, (2) they will follow directions, and (3) they can solve the kinds of problems that might arise in your absence, then it's time to find out what they know about being in charge of themselves. Use the quiz on page 196 to test your child's readiness.

Can Your Child Answer These Questions?

1. Why should you always walk with friends?
2. What should you do if someone is following you?
3. Where should you keep your key?
4. If someone knocks on the door and wants to come into the house, what should you do?
5. When you are alone and someone calls and asks to talk to your parents, what should you do?
6. In case of an emergency, what number should you call?
7. What are the first two things you should do if a fire starts in your house?
8. Before you enter your home, what should you check for?
9. What would you do if you walked into the house and it looked like someone else had been there?

Adapted from *Home Alone*, American Red Cross, Greater Kansas City Chapter, © 1984, 1993.

Make a note of their answers and use them as a baseline for what you need to teach. You should realize that this short quiz doesn't cover all the information your children will need to know before you leave them in charge.

Some of the personal-safety skills that all grade-school children should know are even more important for kids who are expected to care for themselves after school. They are:

- Interacting with strangers
- Using a code word
- Being able to call 911 or 0 to ask for help
- Answering the phone and the door safely
- Being alert and aware of their surroundings

To those skills add fire prevention and fire safety, general first aid, and household problems like blackouts or broken pipes, as well as emergency procedures to follow if they can't reach you. There is no doubt about it: It takes a comprehensive training effort to prepare your children to safely manage on their own, even for only a few hours a day.

GENERAL GUIDELINES

Here are some guidelines that will help you set up a productive after-school arrangement with your children.

- Your goal for children left in charge at home is to reinforce their sense of independence and competence. To accomplish this, you must set up procedures and guidelines that minimize their fear and anxiety, as well as offer emotional support. Above all, you must retain the final authority in most situations and stay in charge as parents.
- Kids on their own are more at risk and should be taught how to handle specific emergency situations. They should also demonstrate that they can handle the responsibilities you give them. If they can't—whether it's cooking, shopping, or baby-sitting—give them more time and practice, and provide supervision until they can manage without your help.
- A child under the age of ten is too young to take care of younger brothers and sisters. Children younger than six should not be left with older siblings.
- Television is not a good baby-sitter. Studies prove that children who watch four or more hours each day become passive and sometimes develop stress and do poorly in school.
- Anticipate your children's needs in your absence and create systems that support their being productive. Organize your home so that things are easy for your children to manage. Rearrange your pantries, refrigerators, and cleaning supplies so that children can easily reach what they need. Set up a work space for homework and projects.
- Three hours is probably the limit for children to be on their own. Start by testing out your children's readiness.

Have them stay alone for a few hours on weekends to prove that they can handle themselves without constant adult supervision.

- If your child will be in charge of other children, enroll him or her in a baby-sitting course. The one I know about is Safe Sitters, a fifteen-hour course offered to children from eleven to fifteen years of age. The cost is forty to fifty dollars.

- Safe Sitters is taught throughout the United States and is recognized by the American Academy of Pediatrics. It covers the basics of child development and infant and child care. Children get hands-on instruction in rescue breathing and basic first aid. Also covered is how and where to get emergency help fast and who to call in case of an accident, a prowler, or a power failure. If your children will be baby-sitting outside of your family soon, they will get useful information about fee setting, screening jobs for safety, and how to have more fun with kids.

SETTING UP THE RULES WITH YOUR KIDS

Each family should develop its own set of home-alone rules. Involve your children in planning to gain their cooperation from the start. Here are some of the issues you need to discuss as you set rules for children in charge of themselves:

- Would you allow your child to have a friend over? Which friends and for how long?
- Is your child allowed to leave the house? For how long? Should he call you before he goes out?
- How do you want her to handle answering the door? Should she talk to people who come to the door, or do you prefer that she not let anyone know she is home? Will your rule be not to let anyone into the house, or will she have a list of safe people she may let in?
- What responsibilities will your child have for younger brothers and sisters?
- What will be expected regarding homework and chores?

Keep the rules consistent but flexible. Review them periodically to allow for your child's growing sense of responsibility and independence. Remember that children will be more willing to follow rules that they have helped make.

NONNEGOTIABLE RULES

There are also some rules and safety policies that are not up to your child to decide. Make a clear distinction between these rules and those that are open to review and revision. Here are the nonnegotiable safety rules to give children who are going to be left in charge:

- When you walk down the street, keep your keys out of sight.
- When you get to the door, open it immediately, go in, and lock the door from the inside.
- Call me or leave a message as soon as you get home from school. Call our backup person—a neighbor or relative who lives close by—if you can't reach me at work.
- If a stranger comes to the door and says there's an emergency, you should call 911, but do not allow the person to come in.
- If a person in uniform comes to the door and says he is the police, call 911. The dispatcher can quickly tell you if an officer has been sent to your address. If the police haven't sent the person, the dispatcher can send a real officer to help you.
- Only answer telephone calls from people you know. Screen *all* calls first using the answering machine. (If you allow your child to talk on the phone, add call waiting, so that you can get through at any time.)

EMERGENCY PROCEDURES

Make a set of emergency procedures and backup systems. Review and update them once or twice a year. Put all emergency information on a bulletin board—let your children design it. Post lists of important phone numbers near every phone in the house.

RESPONSIBILITIES AND ACTIVITIES

In your first discussion about how your child will spend her hours at home, find out what she's comfortable doing as well as what she's not comfortable doing. Every child should be expected to perform some age-appropriate chores and assume daily responsibilities at home. Kids need to feel like they are contributing members of the family.

Map out the family's work, school, and home responsibilities for each week. Children will want to know when each family member will return home and where other siblings are if they aren't home after school. Start with a daily schedule and then graduate to a weekly schedule as children get older. Structuring your children's day or week is one way to turn their free time into productive time.

Involve your child in family planning. Discussions in which you devote time to family activities, routines, and problems help children know you are concerned about their well-being. Brainstorming and problem-solving sessions also help your child develop self-confidence and good judgment.

Help organize your kids' time. Keep current lists of favorite activities and provide the necessary materials for hobbies. Make sure they have books to read and set up a work space for homework and creative projects. Tell them you'll supply pencils and art supplies if they will supply the imagination.

REVIEW AND EVALUATE

Besides reviewing safety rules and procedures on a regular basis, sit down and talk with your children about how they feel about being home alone. They may need a chance to express some worry or even some anger. Truly listen and take what they say seriously. During these discussions evaluate how your child is doing by asking:

- Are you comfortable when you are home alone?
- Do you feel afraid or anxious sometimes? About what?
- How do you entertain yourself? Do you get lonely sometimes?

Discuss that no matter how old they are, it's natural to feel a little lonely or scared at times when they are home alone. Explore the various ways of dealing positively with these natural emotions.

In addition to your efforts, there are community programs that prepare kids to stay home alone. The Red Cross offers a good program, although it is not available in all areas of the country. Call your local child-care and referral center or ask your school for more information. Also, I've listed some books in the Resources section. You may find these at your library or bookstore or send for them by mail.

When It's Not Working

The home-alone arrangement is not for everyone. And, even if it worked one year, children may have difficulty with it the next. Here are some warning signs to look for, behaviors that signal a need for more parental involvement and, possibly, family counseling.

- If your child is unwilling to abide by the family rules and begins lying to you, she cannot be home alone. Also, if she is ignoring or failing assigned responsibilities for the house or other children, she is not ready to be home alone. Find out what's going on and seek alternate arrangements in the meantime.
- If his school grades drop and he withdraws from activities and people who were once important, be concerned. This may be a sign of depression or drug use. Sometimes at this age a child may be participating in forbidden activities like sex or drugs and alcohol. When confronted, he won't tell the truth because he doesn't want to give up the for-

bidden activities completely. He may enjoy some of them, particularly if he is made to feel important or grown up. Or, he may fear that if he told you what was going on, you would restrict his freedom or supervise him constantly. Reassure your child that he will not be punished for revealing secrets to you and that if something is going on that you don't approve of, you won't overreact by keeping him under lock and key. By taking a moderate approach, you have a better chance of hearing about suspicious or illegal activity directly from him.

Key Points

- It's essential to review and update personal safety skills as your children get older.
- Prepare your preteen for new situations that may require more information, awareness, and skill using "What if . . . ?" discussions. Safety review and/or practice is needed before your preteen goes anywhere unsupervised.
- When your preteen demonstrates his or her ability to act responsibly, encourage and reward responsible behavior by granting more privileges.
- Kids in charge of themselves are more at risk and need additional training, emotional support, and monitoring.

CHAPTER 12

What to Do If Your Child Is Molested or Abducted

In the previous chapters, we covered a number of preventive strategies you can teach your children that will protect them from abductors and molesters. If you teach them to be strong and street-smart, your children have a much better chance of navigating their childhoods safely. But, because there remains the small possibility that your child will be molested or abducted despite your best efforts, it's important that you know what steps to take afterward.

Not All Incidents Are the Same

Let's start with how to respond to a single random incident. We'll use the example of a man who sits next to your son in a movie theater and tries to use your child's hand, instead of his own, for masturbation. If your son reports an incident of this kind to you, show concern, but try not to overreact. Your reaction is important and will influence the likelihood of his telling you the next time a similar incident takes place. Explain to him that some people find unknown children sexually exciting, and that these people are sick.

"A child will be less shocked by an adult behaving in such an incomprehensible way if he already knows that some people do peculiar things," says Penelope Leach. "Generally, it is best to respond to a single such incident matter-of-factly." Calmly report the matter to the police and the school, and reassure your child that he was not then—and is not now—in any real danger. Review safety behavior for the next time he is in that or a similar situation. Remember, ongoing relationships *not* random incidents hold the greatest dangers for children. Relationships with trusted friends or family members who exploit the children's trust and that involve repeated molestation are far more damaging.

Effects of Sexual Abuse

According to Carolyn Moore Newberger, the director of the Victim Recovery Study at Children's Hospital in Boston, the effects of child sexual abuse can range from little or no apparent distress to disabling psychological harm. When the "abuse is chronic, when the perpetrator is a family member, when secrecy is coerced, and when force or terror is used, children suffer greater emotional damage." Newberger also notes that if "the abuse leaves the child feeling powerless, betrayed, dirty, or guilty, the trauma is greater than if he or she felt some measure of control or was unaware of being sexually abused."

The age of the child can make a difference as well. The Victim Recovery Study shows that a preschooler fondled by an otherwise loving relative may show no signs of being traumatized. (Sometimes children who were abused when very young develop symptoms years later, after they come to understand what was done to them.) An older child who knows that such touching is wrong and is unable to stop it might develop nightmares, fears of being left alone, or other psychological symptoms.

Sometimes difficulties emerge as children enter new developmental periods. For example, a seven-year-old—abused as a preschooler—starts to talk about being "bad" as he views himself and others. Or, a sexually abused girl may withdraw from boy-girl relationships or jump prematurely into sexual contact. These are misguided attempts to cope with new issues raised by her sexuality.

From the First Phone Call to Court

Experts suspect that many incidents of sexual abuse go unreported—some because of a desire to protect a child from further trauma, and others because of embarrassment or denial. But dramatic changes in laws and in attitudes about child sexual abuse and the growth of victim-assistance programs are helping children manage the maze of social service and criminal justice systems with as little stress and trauma as possible.

Once you report sexual abuse to the police, expect a visit from detectives trained to investigate sex crimes and/or a local or state social-service caseworker. The child will be questioned and examined for visual signs of physical abuse. The investigators may require that the child go to a hospital for a medical examination, and AIDS testing is done in rape cases.

In the case of physical injury or rape, the first priority is to consult a physician. Use your regular pediatrician or family physician, if possible. Whatever medical help you receive, a parent—preferably of the same sex—should stay with a child during any examination and during treatment if it is needed. Parents should reassure the child throughout the exam that he or she will be fine.

You may need to explain what's happening during an exam of the genital or rectal area. You might say, "She's checking to make sure that everything is OK." And whatever the doctor finds, emphasize that this evidence is neither "good" nor "bad." It will simply help the police. Also, if there is any physical damage to be mended, a parent should offer a reassuring, honest, and realistic explanation of what to expect. Say something like

"This may hurt, but I'm right here" or "You may be uncomfortable for a while, but your bottom will feel better very soon."

The fact that children and families are subjected to a labyrinth of people, questions, and procedures has been criticized. Steps are being taken to ease the toll on victims by having social workers, prosecutors, law enforcement officials, doctors, and mental health professionals work as a team. The National Children's Advocacy Center in Huntsville, Alabama, developed a model program that is now copied by sixty-two cities nationwide. They introduced the idea of using one-way mirrors to insure that the child is not surrounded by a lot of people during the interview process. The center also provides therapists who help families make the transition from crisis counseling to ongoing treatment.

Judges in at least thirty states now give priority to court cases involving young child victims. And most states try to keep the identity of the child as confidential as possible. During the process from arrest to trial, which takes from ninety days to two years, witness counselors in prosecutors' offices and crisis centers act as a buffer between the legal system and the victim. They provide three important services: They connect families with therapy and support groups; they help in practical matters like filling out crime-victims compensation papers; and they help prepare the child who must appear in court.

Some jurisdictions take pains to demystify the courtroom. Some district attorneys' offices offer a chance for children to playact the courtroom scene beforehand: Children pretend to be a judge or bailiff in an empty or mock courtroom. Other modifications of traditional courtroom procedures are now offered to children who testify. Some can testify from the security of a parent's or a grandparent's lap. Judges in more than half of the states permit videotaped testimony. The use of closed-circuit television, which shields a child from having to tell her story before the defendant, is still under debate. It is permitted in some courtrooms but has been ruled as inadmissible testimony in others.

The main reasons to prosecute a sex offender is to get him off the streets and to help children regain control of their lives. In sharing his or her terrible secret and realizing that none of the horrifying threats came true, the child gains psychological power over the offender. The secret loses its force and the child's fears are greatly reduced. Although public disclosure and going to court are never easy experiences, mental health professionals who have seen many abuse cases through legal action say that most young victims emerge without further emotional damage being done.

Your Reaction Counts

If your child is sexually molested, it's hard to know exactly how you would react. But, most likely, staying calm would not be your first reaction. Graeme Hanson, M.D., a psychiatrist and child-abuse expert at the University of California, San Francisco, says that parents need to keep some semblance of calm and do whatever they can to control their reactions at home. When a parent becomes overwhelmed, a child may decide not to disclose any more information about the molestation in order to spare his or her parent's feelings, cautions Hanson.

Parents must cope with their own feelings of rage toward the perpetrator and probably also with some irrational guilt for their failure to protect the child. And children must not feel that they are the target of their parents' anger. If parents inadvertently give the impression that their rage is directed toward the child, she can even be made to feel like the perpetrator.

Remember, your child has lived through a frightening and perhaps incomprehensible experience. She is embarrassed at the least, probably humiliated, and may wonder if some weakness on her part was responsible for what happened. The most well-known reaction is kids' belief that they somehow caused the indignity. To make sure your child understands that she is not responsible for what happened, consciously channel your feelings of anger and guilt away from her. Your misdirected anger may make her feel at fault. Your guilt may confuse her and make her feel even more insecure than she does already.

A child's recovery from molestation depends in large part on how well his or her parents cope. If parents can deal with the issues that sexually abused children face, their children will recover sooner and more completely.

When to Seek Help

How can parents help children avoid permanent emotional trauma in the wake of sexual molestation? Should the child be rushed to a psychiatrist or a psychologist? Should parents go into therapy?

Most experts feel that therapy is not automatically indicated. However, many parents in these circumstances find it helpful to talk to a good confidant, family doctor, or therapist about their painful and sometimes overwhelming feelings. After all, they are the secondary victims of child molestation. Parents need to unburden themselves of their feelings about the situation for their emotional well-being so that they can find the right words to comfort their child.

For mothers who were past victims of sexual abuse or rape, a special set of problems exists. These mothers may need help sorting out and working through their own unresolved feelings before they can help their daughters. In many cases, memories and feelings that had been "set aside" are stirred up when their own daughters are molested. Often, sexual abuse continues to be passed on from one generation to the next until either the parent or the child gets help.

For psychologically healthy parents, Dr. Hanson predicts the strongest, most anguished feelings will fade within three to five months after a molestation. But any semblance of feeling normal again may take a year or two. Even then, he says, some feelings of guilt and rage connected with the attack will remain.

Children can exhibit a variety of symptoms in the wake of sexual abuse. Here are some physical signs that a child has been abused:

Pain or irritation in the genital area
Difficulty walking or sitting
Unexplainable injuries and bruises
Frequent bathing
Frequent urination

In addition, there are behavioral signs, some of which may need to be treated by an experienced, sensitive clinician. If disturbing aftereffects continue for longer than a month, or if the child's behavior changes radically, there may be a more serious problem. Here are some typical behaviors exhibited by victims of sexual abuse:

Sleep disturances	Clinging	Increased
Destructiveness	Passivity	nightmares
Depression	Bed-wetting	Precocious sexual
Changes in	Social isolation	information
appetite	Inappropriate	Changes in self-
Irritability	expressions of	image
Suddenly turning	affection	Regressive/
against one	New and increased	immature
parent	fears	behavior

Some of these behaviors may appear shortly after the sexual abuse has occurred. Some may not appear for several months or even years after the molestation. Be alert to sudden or prolonged changes in behavior like those described above and, by all means, investigate them. Children cannot always directly tell us when something unpleasant has occurred. Instead, they will exhibit behavior changes that signal an urgent need for help and understanding.

In the case of a family whose two children were molested by a teenage boy, the parents and the pediatrician looked for plausible explanations. The doctor diagnosed the boy's weepiness at school, his low tolerance for frustration, his bleak outlook, and his refusal to get out of bed in the morning as kindergarten stress. The sister's strong dislike of her new bed and of their house was written off as two-year-old negativity. Her sudden bedtime battles and nighttime waking were blamed on a delayed reaction to the mother's return to work nine months earlier.

Use your parental instincts. If you think something else is wrong, it probably is. To evaluate whether negative or fearful behavior is the result of sexual abuse, consult a therapist with expertise in sexual abuse issues. Your pediatrician may be able to recommend one. Also, you can get referrals from hospitals, mental health clinics, and rape crisis centers.

One of the advantages our children have is that they live in an era when sexual abuse can be spoken about and believed. We know more than ever before about how to help children recover from sexual abuse. There is help available to children and their parents in nearly every community around the United States.

There is only one situation for which I feel therapy should be sought in every case: when your son or daughter is raped in childhood. Therapy received before the onset of adolescence can provide emotional insurance against further complications during the turbulent teen years ahead. However, I don't believe in forcing children into therapy. So, if your child resists going, find out why. Sometimes finding another therapist is the answer.

When you are considering seeking treatment for sexual abuse that occurred last week, last month, or twenty years ago, remember that there is no statute of limitations on healing. You or your child can profit from therapy at any time. A child victimized at age three can benefit from treatment at age ten. A forty-five-year-old adult can resolve a molestation that occurred when he was fourteen.

How Parents Can Help

When parents are at the point where they can respond to their child without letting their own rage and guilt interfere, they should gently try to get a full report of what happened. Encourage him or her to talk about the incident, but without pressure. You can say something like "I'm here to listen whenever you feel like talking about it." It's important not to grill a child, but to listen carefully and show thoughtful concern.

In the earlier example where two children were molested by a teenage boy, the five-year-old victim recounted every detail on a single day. His two-year-old sister, on the other hand, needed the better part of a year to tell her story. The girl began with the least frightening act and ended with the most horrible, a pattern that is classic for molestation victims.

Remember that in most cases the child has not been suddenly or violently attacked. Usually, there has been some kind of friendly overture. Only later did what started as casual touching or a playful game turn into forced sexual contact. Your child may feel confused and even disappointed that the relationship with the adult must come to an end.

If your child experiences nightmares following the incident— a common reaction to a distressing event—you can comfort him or her by saying that "sometimes things that are bothering us come out as scary dreams at night." Also reassure the child that the nightmares will go away.

Often a child becomes particularly sensitive about the body part that has been molested. This is common and nothing to be seriously worried about. If your child feels awkward about touching the sensitive area or having anyone else touch it, be sympathetic and tactful. Acknowledge his feelings by saying, "I can see you feel uncomfortable." Reassure the child that these feelings will pass and that there has been no lasting harm.

The damage of molestation can be short-term if the child has the opportunity to express the experience. Given proper support from sympathetic parents, the child recovers and in many cases remembers the incident as unpleasant rather than traumatic.

WHY CHILDREN TELL—OR STAY SILENT

Barriers to Disclosure— Why Children Don't Tell

- Children feel responsible— as partners, not as victims.
- Children fear disbelief from adults.
- Children believe threats from the offender.
- Children avoid disappointing adults by reporting something repulsive.
- Children resist talking about "nasty" things.
- Children are handicapped in knowing how to describe what has happened to them.
- Children are taught not to "tattle."
- Children are taught to be respectful of adults. Children fear getting an adult into trouble or disobeying an adult who has requested secrecy.

Breaking Barriers— Why Children Tell

- Children tell when they come into contact with someone who appears to "already know."
- Children tell when they come into contact with a confident person who does not appear to be judgmental, critical, or threatening.
- Children tell when they believe a continuation of the abuse will be unbearable.
- Children tell when physical injury occurs.
- Children tell when they receive abuse prevention information.
- Children tell to protect another child.
- Children tell if pregnancy is a threat.
- Children tell when they come into contact with someone who may protect them.

Source: CALM (Child Abuse Listening Mediation), Santa Barbara, California, 1993.

When Your Child Is Missing

While abduction by a parent is by far the most common, the abductions that pose the greatest danger to a child's life—the ones that scare parents most—involve violent criminals. In the case of a criminal abduction, every minute counts. Call the authorities the moment you perceive that your child is lost.

It's important that as soon as you notify the police, you enlist the help of your neighbors and your child's friends, particularly older children. They know your child, can recognize him from a distance, and may also know some places to look for him that you don't know about. Do the initial search yourself and be sure to go door-to-door. Often someone has seen something that will give you an important clue.

But before you expand your search into the neighborhood, be sure to check every room in your house, including under beds and behind the furniture, just in case your child may have fallen asleep in an unusual spot. Then go out and check every house and building in the neighborhood. Look for empty cartons and abandoned refrigerators, washers, and dryers. Someone who knows the child should stay at home in case he or she returns. Also keep a phone line open at all times, in case the child tries to call.

Police may want you to explain why you don't think your child has run away. Think about any reason your child might have for leaving home. If you suspect your child may have left on his own, be sure to share this information with the police. Then file a missing person's report and request that that information be submitted to the National Crime Information Computer (NCIC).

Now is when you'll need the identification kit that you assembled in case of an emergency (see chapter 9). The police will need a recent photo, a detailed physical description of your child, a description of the clothing he or she was wearing, and the name of the last place the child was going to, coming from, or seen at.

Activate a community and state-wide effort to locate your child quickly. Mobilize everyone you know and use your most powerful contacts in the community to put some "muscle" behind the search for your child. As you form your search team, don't overlook the fire department. They, too, can be enlisted to help.

Get the word out through the media; give interviews to local radio and TV stations or newspapers. Contact the newspaper and ask for the city desk editor. Call your TV and radio stations and ask for the producer or station manager. Stress that there is a very small window of time in which your child will be relatively safe, particularly if he or she has been abducted by a criminal.

It's important that you don't launch these all-out efforts until you're sure your child is in danger. Misplacing a child for an hour or two is a frightening ordeal. But if you initiate a full-scale search only to find your toddler asleep underneath a pile of laundry while your house is surrounded by police, neighbors, and news trucks, you're going to feel more than a little embarrassed.

After twenty-four hours, print posters or flyers, being careful about not giving your home address and phone number to avoid extortion threats and crank calls. Local foundations or agencies for missing children in your area often send volunteers to help answer phone calls or to help you organize your mailing and flyer distribution. Call them if they don't contact you. You may also wish to contact the National Center for Missing and Exploited Children at 1-800-843-5678.

Key Points

- Believe the child. Children rarely make up stories about being sexually abused.
- Assure the child that the abuse is not her fault.
- Report the abuse to the proper authorities.
- Have the child examined by a physician to rule out or confirm injury and also for documentation if you will be pressing charges.
- Respond to the child's fear with concern and support.

- Allow the child to talk about the incident(s) without pressuring him or her to do so.
- Do not blame or punish your child for the actions of others.
- Do not create the impression that your child has done something "bad."
- Provide assurance of your support and love.
- Obtain medical attention and counseling for the child, particularly in the case of rape, or when post-traumatic symptoms do not diminish in time.
- If your child is missing, determine every possible reason, then call the police if you feel the child is in danger.
- Call the police followed by your neighbors, friends, community, and the media. Your actions in the first twenty-four hours are critical.

Conclusion

Concern over our children's safety has grown tremendously in the past decade. Today, a groundswell of support for legislative action is building. Laws carrying more stringent sentences for convicted felons are being debated around the country. And, in some states like California, they are already in place. Increased and more sophisticated methods of monitoring the whereabouts of sex offenders are being developed by law enforcement agencies at the local, state, and federal levels.

But as parents, we can't wait for new laws to be enacted or for new systems to be put in place. Teachers, child-care providers, youth leaders, clergy, law enforcement officers, and other concerned adults must step forward and do their share. With crime what it is, parents cannot take total responsibility for ensuring their children's safety.

Now, more than ever, there are opportunities to take an active interest in making life safer for our children, whether it is in our families, in our neighborhoods, or in our communities. For example, as a parent you can ask your PTA to sponsor a safety assembly at your child's school. School programs about safety can be excellent additions to the information you present to your children. I recommend that elementary schools offer separate safety presentations for lower and upper grades and that once a year they offer a program for parents alone or for parents with their children. This ensures that parents get some information and support on how to teach personal safety at home.

While the community and schools now provide some safety information, there are still parents who do not know how to provide their children with information and safe home environments or are unable to do so. We can do more to reduce the victimization of children if we are willing to keep an eye out for *all* kids, not just our own.

You can establish a Block Parent program that selects "safe houses" as places children can go to if they need immediate help or are frightened. This program is well suited for today's neighborhoods, where people are less likely to see or know one another. All volunteers are screened by law enforcement officials before they are given a special placard to identify their homes as havens for children in distress. For more information about how to set up this program, contact the National Crime Prevention Council in Washington, D.C. I also recommend starting Neighborhood Watch programs to give families a greater sense of control over their streets, particularly in high-crime areas.

Even as communities step forward to provide protection, information, or training, parents must maintain an active, ongoing teaching role with their children. There is no one better place to empower a child with knowledge and confidence than at home. A family atmosphere that encourages open communication, teaches personal safety, and promotes self-esteem is ideal for helping kids become both confident and careful.

Too many parents—and some professionals—believe that children will be more frightened if they are taught about sexual abuse and abduction. This is simply not true. Preventive strategies presented in a matter-of-fact and reassuring manner do not scare children. On the other hand, alarming words and phrases do. The emotional tone of the message—more than the information itself—determines how well children hear, remember, and use safety information.

When it comes to their children's safety, however, many parents become fearful or overwhelmed. They spill their fears and worries into safety conversations with their kids while mistakenly thinking they are teaching them how to avoid the ploys of molesters and kidnappers. We must avoid scare tactics that generate fear and insecurity.

In talking with your children:

- Be realistic about dangers; don't over- or understate them in conversations with your children.
- Monitor the words and phrases you use.
- Use language that is nonalarming.
- Use a matter-of-fact tone of voice.
- Notice the expression on your face.
- Teach specific things your children can do rather than what they should *not* do.
- Reassure children; promise support and protection.

Self-awareness and conscious discipline are the keys to dealing with your own feelings apart from your conversations with your children. And yet, as parents and adults, we all have issues that stem from our childhoods, perhaps painful experiences that may interfere with our ability to nurture and support our children. It takes considerable effort to stay aware of our personal issues and not pass them on to our children, intentionally or otherwise. The best insurance we have against contaminating our parenting and teaching efforts with our own problems is awareness, adult support, and, perhaps, counseling.

Another way we can prevent our children from becoming stressed or overly fearful is to limit their exposure to the news and TV docudramas that offer vivid and often violent depictions of crime. We must serve as gatekeepers of the world's problems for our children. It is our job to see that their sense of security isn't damaged by sensationalized reports of crime and violence on television and in the newspapers.

Throughout this book, I've encouraged you to examine how

to protect your children and to strive for some balance between sheltering them completely and being overly optimistic about their ability to handle freedom. Without a doubt, making wise decisions about your child's ability to safely handle situations is a challenge. But, by using common-sense approaches grounded in age-appropriate information, you are likely to be successful. Identify your child's abilities—verbal and social, intellectual and emotional—and use that information to set specific safety rules that are geared to his or her strengths and weaknesses.

Give children the kind of freedom that allows them to develop into resourceful problem solvers and confident kids. Don't shelter them from experiences that will help them become more self-reliant, even if they experience some emotional pain along the way. At the same time, we must not hand our young people more responsibility than they can safely manage. And, no child should be left home alone who is either afraid or unprepared to be in charge of himself and/or others.

Ongoing dialogue that begins at an early age combined with short and simple learning activities provide the structure for how you can effectively present safety issues at home. Teaching personal safety is a continuous process that takes on new information and requires new approaches as your children grow and change. With each new developmental stage and with each new challenge, you must reevaluate your children's level of preparedness.

You start in the preschool years by establishing family safety rules and procedures. You provide close supervision while your children learn how to identify their body parts and communicate their feelings. In grade school, you teach kids a variety of safety skills and encourage them to develop and trust their instincts about people and situations. Then, as they enter their preteen years, you discuss more complex issues such as rape, as well as the important differences between sexuality and sexual abuse. As your children demonstrate their ability to use and remember street-smart skills, you begin to loosen the reins little by little as they enter their teen years.

One point I stressed in this book is that busy parents can use simple and direct techniques for teaching safety during their natural routines and conversations. The safety training you do at home doesn't need to add to or override your other activities. It can be included in them. You can make personal safety an integrated part of your family's life by looking for and using teachable moments throughout the day. The best approach is to teach a little bit at a time over time, using a relaxed but conscious effort. Also, to stimulate your children's interest and make learning fun, allow yourself to be playful and creative about how you teach personal safety. Your kids will love you for it, and the quality of time you spend together will be enhanced.

In addition to the many duties you already have as parents and providers, I'm asking you to create a nurturing and secure home environment and to provide the safety knowledge and practice your children need. I know this may feel like a tall order. The risks involved with raising children today require us to make these efforts. We have the added task of teaching our kids to be aware of the potential dangers in their environment, while at the same time promoting their growth, independence, and high self-esteem.

You are now—and will always be—your child's most important teacher. You have a day-to-day understanding of your child's likes, dislikes, abilities, and communication styles, all of which help you do your job more effectively. Most likely, you are the first one to notice a change or a problem. By increasing your awareness as a parent and by acting on your instincts to teach and prepare your children, you become a protective parent and a highly effective teacher of personal safety.

I believe that our children benefit immeasurably from our involvement and teaching efforts. For one thing, they feel that they are worthy of our time and attention. For another, they see that they are loved and cherished. A molester is no match for a child who feels worthwhile and loved.

Our message to kids must be that they can take precautions to protect themselves against crime. Ultimately, we want our children to know they have some control over their environment and their bodies and that they don't have to be victimized by others. Such an empowering message comes across by our example, our words, and our positive and direct action.

I cannot imagine a better gift to give children growing up in these difficult times than enabling them to feel secure in themselves and their abilities to cope with any dangers they may face. By reading this book and by using these suggestions at home with your children, you will be able to give them the confidence and skill they need. Plus, you will have the pride in knowing that you handled this extremely important parental task with confidence and courage.

Dear Reader,

I hope you found the insights and ideas in this book valuable. I would enjoy hearing your comments, questions, and your own experiences—especially success stories—arising from your use of the suggestions in this book.
I also have available:

- a lecture and a workshop on which this book is based
- a number of other parent education programs, as well as workshops for women
- a selection of audio and video programs expanding upon women's and parents' issues
- KidWISE Instructor Certification Training

For information on Paula's availability for speeches and workshops, for product information, to learn about the KidWISE Instructor Certification program, or to receive her newsletter, KidWISE Corner, please contact:

KidWISE Institute, Inc.
484 Lake Park Ave. #101
Oakland, CA 94610-2730
510-444-8721or 888-KidWISE
fax: 510-465-7259
pnstatman@aol.com
or
visit our web site at
http://www.KidWISEInstitute.com